DESTINY

ALSO BY T.D. JAKES

Instinct

Reposition Yourself

Maximize the Moment

64 Lessons for a Life Without Limits

Making Great Decisions

The T.D. Jakes Relationship Bible

The Great Investment

The Ten Commandments of Working in a Hostile Environment

On the Seventh Day

Not Easily Broken

So You Call Yourself a Man?

Woman, Thou Art Loosed!

He-Motions

Mama Made the Difference

God's Leading Lady

Can You Stand to Be Blessed?

Let It Go

DESTINY

Step into Your Purpose

T.D. Jakes

FaithWords

New York Boston Nashville

FaithWords
Hachette Book Group
1290 Avenue of the Americas
New York, NY 10104

www.faithwords.com

Printed in the United States of America

RRD-C

First Edition: August 2015
10 9 8 7 6 5 4 3 2 1

FaithWords is a division of Hachette Book Group, Inc.
The FaithWords name and logo are trademarks of Hachette Book Group, Inc.

The Hachette Speakers Bureau provides a wide range of authors for speaking events. To find out more, go to www.hachettespeakersbureau.com or call (866) 376-6591.

The publisher is not responsible for websites (or their content) that are not owned by the publisher.

Library of Congress Cataloging-in-Publication Data

Jakes, T. D.
Destiny : step into your purpose / T.D. Jakes. — First Edition.
pages cm
Includes index.
ISBN 978-1-4555-5397-6 (hardcover) — ISBN 978-1-4555-8963-0 (large print) — ISBN 978-1-4789-0432-8 (audio download) — ISBN 978-1-4555-5398-3 (ebook)
1. Self-actualization (Psychology)—Religious aspects—Christianity. 2. Vocation—Christianity. 3. Fate and fatalism—Religious aspects—Christianity. I. Title.
BV4598.2.J36 2015
248.4—dc23

2015017111

ISBN 978-1-4555-8875-6 (international trade)
ISBN 978-1-4555-3851-5 (autographed edition)
ISBN 978-1-4555-3850-8 (B&N autographed edition)

I would like to dedicate Destiny *to the TDJ Enterprises staff and team, who allowed me to learn to lead while leading them. To the Potter's House family—your hunger to know drove me to dig deeper in life. To my many friends who challenged me, inspired me, prayed for me, and encouraged me along the way. I always tried to make sure you knew who you were and your value to me.*

To my loving wife, Serita, and my five gifted children, Jamar, Jermaine, Cora, Sarah, and Dexter. To my siblings, Ernest and Jacqueline. You are all my family, I love you dearly! I've learned so much from you all about life and love and what matters most. I'm sure I couldn't have survived without you giving me a reason to grow on! Thank you for giving me the gift of having you in my life!

Contents

CHAPTER 1: Instinct Plus Purpose Equals Destiny 1

Step beyond Instinct

- Instinct Is Only the First Step
- *Why* Is de Elephant "Ova Dere"?
- Feel the Rhythm of Instinct to Connect to Your Authentic Self
- Instinct Must Merge with Purpose to Find Destiny
- Move from Intention to Inception
- First Draw Internally
- Steer toward Destiny
- Destiny Awaits You

CHAPTER 2: There *Is* More 19

Step toward Greater Fulfillment and Purpose

- What Does More Look Like?
- More Beyond What You Can See Right Now
- Discover *Plus Ultra* Living
- You Can't Win Just Playing Offense
- Get Inspired by People Who Help You Spiral Up
- Imbalances in Our Lives Can Create Frustration
- Use What You Have to Help You Soar

CHAPTER 3: Order Your Steps toward Destiny 33

Choose What's Important to You

- Respect Steps, Establish Order
- Have Patience with the Process
- Prioritize, Focus, Ignore
- Acquire the Skill of Guiltless Prioritization
- Are You Living Evidence of an Ordered Life?
- Ordering Your Life Takes Time
- It's Never a Convenient Time

CHAPTER 4: Destiny Is Spelled P-R-I-O-R-I-T-I-Z-E 53

Get Your Relationships, Money, and Thoughts in Step with Your Destiny

- Prioritize Your Relationships
- Prioritize Your Finances
- Prioritize What's Important for *You* to Fulfill *Your* Dream
- Cultivate a Great Mind and Leave Behind Small Thinking
- Destiny's Diminutive Beginnings
- Flexibility Keeps You from Breaking

CHAPTER 5: Focus—Decide What Deserves You 71

Step toward What's Worth Your Time and Energy

- Your Gifts Make Room for You
- Destiny Always Pays Its Bills
- Destiny Is Worth Fighting For
- Focus Will Sustain Your Passion
- "You'll Win If You Don't Quit!"
- Storms, Struggles, Battles, and Destiny

CHAPTER 6: For Destiny's Sake, Do You! 85

Take Steps toward Authentic Self-Identity

- You'd Like to Get to Know You
- Put That Down! It's Not Yours, Anyway
- Invest in Doing You!
- You Play the Lead Role in Your Destiny

CHAPTER 7: Maybe It's Time for a Reset 97

Change Your Step to Get in Step with Your Destiny

- Take the Chain Off Your Brain
- How to Reset
- Stay Strong in the Struggle
- You Will Make It through the Storm
- Change Your Mind to a New Normal

CHAPTER 8: Time Flies Even When You're Not Having Fun 115

Take Steps to Protect Your Priceless Commodity

- Every Day Is a Withdrawal from the Bank of Time
- Time Is Priceless
- Mind Your Own Busy-ness
- Beware of the Fast Pursuit of Destiny
- Savor Every Moment in Time
- Destiny Doesn't Retire
- Take Your Eyes Off the Clock
- Don't Die in Your Nest

CHAPTER 9: Keep the Destiny Vision 129

Connect Where You Came from to Where You're Going

- Run the Race with Blinders On

- Destiny Requires Street Cred
- It's Complicated
- Dig Deeper Inside You
- Don't Say, "Don't Go There!"
- Provision for Your Vision
- Understand the Complexity of Destiny
- Don't Stay at the Party Too Long

CHAPTER 10: Put a Stop to What's Stopping You 149

Step Out of Stuck!

- You've Already Got It Going On, Baby!
- From Stuck to Strategy
- Destiny Takes More Than You
- Destiny Requires More Than Luck, Anointing, or Natural Talent

CHAPTER 11: Learn from the Destiny of Others 161

Step into Greater Exposure

- Are You One of the Bootstrap People?
- Mentoring Begins Where Education Ends
- Do You Need a Mentor?
- Take the Tour
- Choose Your Mentors à la Carte

CHAPTER 12: Failure Is Not the End of Destiny 179

Step in Your Mess and See the Value of Your Mistakes

- Get Up Again . . . and Again
- Find Reward in Failure

CHAPTER 13: Destiny Demands a Curious Mind 187

Get in Step with the Pursuit of Greater Knowledge

- Stretch Yourself. Let Go and Learn!
- Forget the Dumb Stuff!
- Feed Your Mind's Cravings
- Inquiring Minds Want to Know More

CHAPTER 14: Distractions Destroy Destiny 199

Step Away from What Doesn't Matter

- Know Why You Seek Destiny
- Destiny Starts in Your Head
- Get in Your Zone

CHAPTER 15: Hear Destiny's Voice 209

Step Aside to Listen for Destiny's Authentic Call

- You Can't Tell Everybody
- An Opinion Is Just That
- Avoid the Deceptive Lure of Popularity
- Don't Listen to People Who Have Nothing to Lose
- Hear the Still, Small Voice of Destiny

CHAPTER 16: Exposed to Destiny 221

Step Boldly into Life's Adventures

- Exposure Is Your Test-Drive for Destiny
- Destiny Comes in Pieces
- Go with the Flow of Destiny
- Look from Destiny's Perspective

CHAPTER 17: Destiny Demands Courage 233

Your Steps Are Unstoppable!

- Don't Let Your Destiny Become a Horror Movie
- What Do You Do When the Theater Lights Go On?
- Make Destiny Decisions
- Elevate Your Mind to Destiny

Acknowledgments 245

Index 247

About the Author 255

DESTINY

CHAPTER 1

Instinct Plus Purpose Equals Destiny

Step beyond Instinct

As I quietly stepped onto the elevator and gently pushed the L button to return to the lobby, the incredible blessing I'd just experienced held me spellbound. On the elevator ride down, I pondered the glimpse into history just shared with me by the legendary Mrs. Coretta Scott King during her last days of health and vitality.

We had enjoyed a lunch in her elegant Atlanta penthouse suite, where she lived during her elder years with dignity and class. As we dined, Mrs. King retold many of her amazing experiences from the bird's-eye perspective of her deepest reflections. The memories she shared were moments I had witnessed only through newsreels and history books.

She guided me down a hallway decorated with gripping images reflecting a life on the edge of death, yet illuminated by passion and conviction. She shared what it was like during her years with the Reverend Dr. Martin Luther King Jr., including many moments of peril. As she recalled heart-wrenching experiences, she spoke with the compassion of a mother—somehow, everyone's mother—and not just the mother of her four enigmatic, intriguing progeny.

One of the many topics we discussed that day was a piercing question I posed, a subject considered taboo by many. I asked her why she never remarried. Before responding, she looked at me as if my question was actually rather foolish. Mrs. King smiled and almost giggled when she responded, "Martin was a tough act to follow." Indeed he must have been. Few men have ever affected the culture, the country, and the world as Dr. King did. But what she said next took my breath away. "I was called to be his wife," she said. "It was my destiny to stand beside him."

This woman, whose legendary singing voice merited a career of its own, whose speaking skills and intellect qualified her for many roles, clearly perceived her destiny. Mrs. King could have been anything she wanted—from university president to entrepreneur—yet she chose to support the civil rights movement, underscoring the mission and keeping alive the dream of her martyred husband! She shared so many experiences about her life, little did I realize she actually was reflecting on them from the posture of her imminent demise. Only in retrospect did I consider her small plate of slowly consumed fruits, and her contentment watching me enjoy the ample offering of culinary delights prepared for me.

Her contented smile betrayed the gravity of her condition, which I knew to be a battle with cancer, and one she would shortly lose. Or did she really lose at all? Her smile taught me the value of contentment with a life well lived, a life that had run its course. Coretta Scott King lived comforted by her belief that despite the turbulence of her journey, she had lived on course with a destiny far more important than the waves of grief and tumult she experienced in the life and in the murder of her husband. She was at peace!

If only you and I could replicate her resolve in our own lives. Could it be that we allow the conditions in our lives to distract us from the meaning of our lives? Is it possible that we don't spend enough time checking the dials and reading the compass of Destiny and its intrinsic pull on the human soul?

If we are wise we will see the predestined purpose we were created for and, in our brief life span, find it and do it. It is my hope that each of us will be free from the purposeless living that causes so many to stumble aimlessly through life.

Like Mrs. King, we all were created to fulfill some role only through which we can find the great elixir of contentment and courage. Whatever the assignment, death loses its license to threaten those who are certain we have lived before we face its clutching grasp.

As the elevator descended the thirty-nine stories to the lobby, I reflected on the fact that I, too, have lived a life to which I felt drawn. I have been pulled by a call that has drawn me from the mundane acquisition of life's mementos to the far more rewarding task of doing something with my life that only I could uniquely accomplish.

Instinct Is Only the First Step

Sometimes we are amazed by what human beings can endure. Looking at the life of Mrs. King, we wonder how she withstood the challenges of raising her children practically alone, the death threats, the bombings, and the relentless FBI probes. What motivates a person to find contentment in a life of struggle, as Nelson Mandela did during his nearly twenty-seven years in a South African prison?

When we watch people fully engaged in their purpose, it's confirmation that God has given each of us a destiny. How else could one person be so fascinated by the accuracy of numbers while another is totally obsessed with the accuracy of words? What allows you to have great interest in something that bores other people to tears? Why are you able to pick up anything and fix it—from a clock to an automobile—while other people should be arrested for even picking up a hammer? Why are you able to devote countless hours to reading a book while other people will never know the story line if it's not on video? The gift or desire that God has wired you to express is unique to you. Others can't understand how you do what you do, but neither can you understand how they act in their gifts.

Why do you get angry when you see certain things not done properly? It's your instinct. You are irritated by the fact that you know it could be done better.

I remember reading a story about an Olympian who was charged with a serious crime. After he was released on bond, the first thing he did was resume his workout routine. As I was reading his story, I thought, "If I were under the public microscope for that kind of crime, no way would I be spending my time working out." But then I considered the fact that this man was a champion athlete, and real champions cannot help but do what they are gifted to do. It is their therapy. It is how they fortify themselves. You are a champion when you overcome adversity and go back to doing what you were doing before.

The drive to do what you're good at is instinct. It's what God has created you to do. The kind of instinct given to God's highest creation is not the same as the instinct that causes a sea turtle to make her way to the ocean shoreline to lay her eggs and then return to sea. Human instinct in action is a pure joy to behold. It's like a work of art in motion, like watching Michael

Jordan dunk a basketball or listening to a hypnotic melody offered by violin virtuoso Itzhak Perlman.

Why Is de Elephant "Ova Dere"?

In my previous book, *Instinct,* we explored how people are wired. That book became a best seller because a great many people are searching for a way to tune in to what God has embedded inside them. I shared my experience of being on an African safari, attended by a zoologist and a guide. I discovered that the zoologist knew everything about the biology and habits of the elephant, but it took the instinct of the safari guide to tell us, "De elephant is ova dere." We found the elephant, but no one on the safari was able to tell us *why* it was "ova dere." The answer lies in God's purpose and plan for creating elephants.

If you're like me, you've experienced times when you wondered, "Why am I here?" You may have asked the question as you found yourself in the midst of an amazing, divinely orchestrated opportunity, or you may have asked it in reaction to having made the worst mistake of your life. You may wonder why you are in a chosen position that was sought by dozens of people with equal or greater qualifications. You may wonder why you went to college but all of your boys ended up dead or in prison. You may wonder why all of your goal-oriented friends have slowly pulled away from you, and now all your time is spent around people who have no goals and don't want you to have any, either. You can know the logistics and mechanics of how you got where you are but still not answer the question why. Without the why, you can never connect to purpose; through purpose you connect to Destiny.

Instinct shared how you are wired and gave strategies to unleash what God has already placed inside you. Instinct is the how, but Destiny reveals *why* you are wired. I felt particularly compelled to write this book because the "why" is always more powerful than the "how" of life. I'm excited about this book as an opportunity to move beyond the how and explore the why. Both connect to direct you to Destiny.

It's a powerful life transition to unleash what lies inside you, but that unleashing only becomes viable when it can be validated by the why. We know how babies are made and, as mystical as the science of procreation can be, we can absorb that miraculous information much easier than the why of life. Why are we born? Why were you born?

One of humanity's central life questions relates to the why of life. All of us have grappled with the question of a personal purpose that confirms our destiny: Why am I here? For some people, the question is little more than a short-lived intellectual pursuit. For others, it is a lifelong quest. Yet the mere fact that the question has been posed through ceaseless generations affirms that there is an internal quest that pricks the human heart. That quest is fueled by humanity's need to know that our efforts and actions are congruent with our passion and purpose.

As we follow the instinctive path of our passion molded into action, we connect to Destiny. As we explore the path to Destiny, we gain a barometer by which we may measure authentic purpose, otherwise known as success. One can't define success in dollars or cents. It can only be quantified by the accomplishment of a predestined purpose! This need to answer the why of life cannot be satiated solely by fame or wealth or notoriety, or even education, as none of these acquisitions guarantees that action has aligned with purpose in our lives.

Destiny is the push of our instincts to the pull of our purpose. That push-pull is what keeps the sun, moon, and stars from crashing. It causes the seasons to change from planting to growing to harvest to dormancy. If that divine push-pull, known as gravity, accurately sets the galaxies and the seasons in motion, will the same principle—the push of instinct and the pull of purpose—not set your life in the right motion? What gravity is to the order of our universe, Destiny is to the meaning of your life.

Feel the Rhythm of Instinct to Connect to Your Authentic Self

Walt Disney's *Cool Runnings* movie is an entertaining, fictionalized account of a Jamaican bobsled team's journey to the Winter Olympics. Their team captain encouraged the novice bobsledders to follow the methodology of the Swiss, who had many more years of experience competing. They tried following the techniques of the Swiss team, but it wasn't working for them. Their performance couldn't qualify them for Olympic competition; that is, until they made the pivotal decision to bobsled like Jamaicans. Their rallying cry became, "Feel the rhythm, feel the rhyme. Get on up, it's bobsled time!" While the Swiss effectively counted themselves into position—"*Eins, zwei, drei*"—the Jamaican competitors finally figured out their strategy: "If we walk Jamaican, talk Jamaican, and *is* Jamaican, then we sure... better bobsled Jamaican!"

The Jamaican Olympians had to learn how to function in their gifts authentically. The problem wasn't that they had no talent for bobsledding; they weren't in touch with their instinct on the matter. In the same way, people must learn to live genuine lives that allow them to perform the life tasks they are gifted to do.

Barbra Streisand and Aretha Franklin are both music icons with tremendous talent. But what if you went to one of Barbra's rare performances and heard her trying to sing like the Queen of Soul? You'd know something was wrong. The performance would not ring authentic.

Entertainers, scholars, preachers, and athletes alike all have admitted to being influenced by the skill and style of someone who came before them. Michael Jackson and Prince were clearly influenced by the performances of the Godfather of Soul, James Brown. Many preachers a generation ago were influenced by the oratorical styles of Martin Luther King Jr. and Billy Graham. Exposure to others who are good at what they do can be highly motivating and instructional; it helps us understand the manifestation of our own gifts. Observing others can help us set the bar of excellence high for ourselves. But there must be a point where one respects, admires, and learns from others, and then turns inward to connect to his or her authentic expression of talent. Robert Frost and Maya Angelou were great poets, but each had a distinctive style. Your instinct will draw you to the unique expression of your gifts.

You can prosper effectively only by drawing on what is authentically in you. The drawing process starts from your core. You can only be fruitful out of your understanding of and connection to what is in your core. In the movie *Ray*, as singer Ray Charles tries to establish a recording sound, he mimics the styles of his contemporaries until he hits upon a style that is uniquely his own. In real life, Charles was criticized for his innovations in music, but he carved out a new blend in music and found his authentic sound.

It can be frightening to own your authentic self. What if other people don't approve of the authentic you? What if they criticize or make fun of who you really are? That's a painful prospect to consider, especially when disapproval or criticism comes from the people who mean the most to you. Are you prepared to brave the negative reactions, comments, criticisms, and complaints that may arise from owning your authentic self? Can you handle it? Some people can't. They live without expressing the authenticity of what abides deep within them because the approval of others is more important to them than self-approval.

Those who live according to what others expect or accept because they do not have the courage to be the person their instinct draws forth from inside are only existing. They really haven't learned how to live. Real life means discovering what God has placed inside you!

God has invested a great deal in you, and for all the Creator has put in you, there is only one thing God wants to know: "What will you do with what I gave you?" God expects you to work excellence at the level given to you. As the late author, professor, and motivational speaker Leo Buscaglia explained it, "Your talent is God's gift to you. What you do with it is your gift back to God."

Instinct Must Merge with Purpose to Find Destiny

Instinct is that inherent aptitude or capacity to use your emergent God-given gifts effectively at the appointed time and place. It's the urging inside you that tells you to make your move now, to reach out now, to hold back until later, or to never give up.

Instinct must merge with purpose to give you a life that fulfills your destiny. All gifts must be given a place of expression in order for Destiny to unfold.

We are most effective when we yield to the allure of destiny! Every gifted person needs a place to engage the gifts that are rooted inside. No matter how gifted you are, you need a place of expression. That place is Destiny.

Your instinctive gifts are the metal inside you. Your destiny is the magnet that draws you to its predestined arena. People who have instinct with no apparent destiny are waiting to be lifted by something higher than what led them to tune in to instinct. We must be drawn by something deeper. Destiny pulls us beyond the familiar toward our future.

Even if you're not a Bible reader, you're probably familiar with the biblical story of Moses at the burning bush. This great leader of Israel was drawn to a bush burning in the wilderness because he noticed the leaves did not burn off. Destiny is the fire that attracts us to come toward her. She ignites our curiosity. Moses' entire world had been turned upside down. He was a fugitive who fell from sultan to shepherd. His traumatic ouster from Egypt helped connect Moses to his instincts. When he was no longer a pampered prince, he got in touch with the gifts and abilities that God had given him to survive a wilderness existence and prosper in a life of hard work caring for a flock of animals—exposure that would be essential to Israel's survival when God used him to deliver Israel from slavery in Egypt.

There at the burning bush was the cross point at which Moses' former life met his future life. It was the place where the instinct that pulled him to the burning bush connected with the destiny that would push him back to Egypt and beyond and connect to his destiny. Like Moses at the burning bush, we may not comprehend why we are thrust beyond our familiar surroundings, but we can trust that we are being drawn by Destiny. Instinct and purpose often operate like a marriage. It's not always a fifty-fifty proposition. Sometimes you may function more from a sense of instinct, while at other times the quest for purpose may have a gale-force wind propelling you forward. But the sometimes unbalanced partners will direct you. When instinct and purpose connect, their progeny is Destiny.

Move from Intention to Inception

If the road to hell is paved with good intentions, the road to heaven is paved with relentless faith. Faith requires the prenatal care of dreams, the nourishment of dream makers, and the feeding of dragon slayers until the abstract becomes concrete.

There are perhaps millions who are sitting on the couch saying, "I'm gonna..." They'll do it when their finances are perfect, when their children are perfectly grown and stable, when they've achieved seniority on the job or some other life marker. Your life will never be perfect. Parts of it will be, at times. You will always be juggling and adjusting in some area of your life. Step away from the couch sitters who are awaiting the single perfect day to begin living their dream. You can choose to live your dream every day if you just take the first step. Every day will not feel dreamy and some may feel like a nightmare, but if you never get off your intentions, your vision for your life may never become a reality. Have enough faith to believe in God and in yourself and know that together the two of you can do anything!

Increase your capacity to receive what is destined to happen if you believe! If you can see the invisible, you can do the impossible. You may have to stretch yourself or enlarge your circle of associates. You may have to expose yourself beyond your comfort zone or speak when you are naturally introverted. Stretch yourself; it's worth it!

Understanding this synergistic connection of instinct with

purpose to give birth to Destiny is important in the life of every individual. Every person has a destiny to fulfill. It is essential to craft an environment that facilitates the fulfillment of Destiny.

First Draw Internally

In the account of creation recorded in the Bible, I am fascinated by a line that most overlook. It says that God created every living thing with a seed inside itself. Wow! Isn't that how all of life is formed? It re-creates from what exists within itself. The seed to achieve comes from the divine thoughtfulness of God, who has prewired us to produce. Your creativity is within you. Your peace and power come from digging beneath your surface and locating your own core of potential.

Our tendency is to look outside ourselves for comfort, happiness, or fulfillment. You may look to a new job to feel successful and worthy. You believe a relationship will bring you a sense of fulfillment and purpose in your life. You buy a new car or a new house, thinking that will impress others and increase your social standing. All of these are wonderful, but all of them depend on people or conditions that are outside of you. Nothing outside of you can make you who you are. It's already in you. God has already implanted in you the raw materials needed to shape Destiny into reality. You already have what's needed to actualize your vision for your life. It is a God-given vision; otherwise, you would not have it.

Think about the fact that since God created the world, nothing new has been created. Many, many devices have been invented, but nothing has been created. Everything that humankind has developed came from what God had already put in or on the earth. Every invention and modern convenience that you enjoy was created out of resources that are already on this earth. Someone simply had the vision to bring it into reality.

Steer toward Destiny

If you think of the human mind as the steering wheel that determines the direction of one's destiny, then we are transforming our lives by the way we turn our minds. You limit yourself when you operate only on an intellectual or psychological level and refuse to pay attention to the spiritual inclinations residing in you.

You can turn your mind to education, but somewhere along the line, even a PhD will leave you lacking. You can turn your mind to logic or reason or common sense or even coincidence in search of life's answers, but all of these will leave you lacking. Tune in to the fact that the instinct pushing out from you and the purpose pulling at you are a part of God's larger plan for you to fulfill your destiny.

Your mind may guide you in what you do, but your heart affirms your passion to do it, and that leads you to resolve the why of your life. Within your passion lies the clue to your deeper purpose—and ultimately, your destiny. As you stand back from yourself to see the push of instincts welded with the pull of purpose that leads you to Destiny, you will know the events and circumstances in your life equate to more than coincidences or mere facts. The coming together of all these events and connections, some seemingly random, are the result of divine orchestration to empower you to accomplish what God has placed you here to do.

Destiny is so much bigger than you. Trust that the results are not in your hands. An encounter with Destiny generally comes only after intentional exposure and heeding the pull of purpose.

Think about a girl or guy you wanted to date. You wanted to impress that person. If you were still in school, you might have updated your wardrobe and started wearing makeup and heels. You might have gotten a part-time job so you could afford to take her out. You did all of that to get that person's attention. You did all of that to show the person you were worthy of getting close to him or her. Show Destiny that you're worth getting close to. Show Destiny that you won't mess up the opportunity to travel in the same circles with her. Destiny is a fastidious companion that is rarely, if ever, stumbled upon. But until you find her, she will tease and taunt you. She will call out to you as you endeavor to discover the why of your life.

Destiny will sometimes be elusive and guide you on a circuitous path as you follow her in search of why. But led by instinct as you pursue purpose, you will discover the why of your life, and then you will know that fulfillment of Destiny is the greatest kind of success you can ever hope to attain.

Destiny Awaits You

Most people have sensed the pull of Destiny's magnet that caused them to meet who they've met, to go where they've been, or to do what they've done. During times of reflection, most of us are amazed to realize that the greatest moments of our lives happened only through a series of circumstances that we ourselves did not initiate. Think about the serendipitous encounters, the synchronous timing of events, and the chance meetings in your life. Had you not been in that restaurant, you never would have met a business contact, a future spouse, or an employer. If you had not attended that summer camp, your fascination with wildlife or biology or botany or sports medicine would have never been spawned.

What orders our steps? To the faithful, it is God alone. The secular may interject words like *fate* or *luck*. Whatever the name, all of us are left drawn by the pull of Destiny's allure.

Ride the wave of life with a sense of guidance to something beyond self-gratification. It adds meaning to life. Do not halt at the rest stop of distraction nor succumb to the indulgent luxury of self-pity. The problems and challenges we face could be merely distractions from the greater force of the destiny that draws us from where we started to where we will accomplish what we were meant to do. If you sense that there is an order to your steps, a guidance that has corrected you when you were off course and nudged you when you sat in a holding pattern too long, then read on.

Destiny awaits. It is always an adventure. It drives us past the pain of life to the purpose of living. There's more going on in your life than just you.

At moments that I felt the least adept, I have known there is a force beneath my wings for which I could take no credit. There was a perfect timing I could not explain. There was a person I could never have schemed to meet. There was an opportunity I could never have orchestrated on my own.

As I waited on the sidewalk of Mrs. King's high-rise development for my car, I remembered that I had spoken at Carlton Pearson's Azusa meeting. I had been a guest speaker at that ministerial conference many years ago, but the sequence of events that surrounded that single invitation to speak still amazes me. After Azusa had ended that year, Pastor Pearson had decided to air clips of the three-day event featuring three preachers. I was only one of the clips he broadcast on his weekly television program on the Trinity Broadcasting Network. The network's founder, Paul Crouch, happened to be watching. The clip of my sermon addressed the vulnerability of showing your wounds to help others with their own. Crouch was writing a book titled *I Had No Father but God*. What I said during that clip inspired him to share aspects of his story that he had wrestled with taking public.

As I stepped into my car to leave Mrs. King's building, I thought that if the late Paul Crouch had walked away from the TV to get a ham sandwich, he never would have seen that brief video clip that moved him to invite me to appear on TBN, and later inspired him to offer me a network time slot. Without owning a camera and with only one person on staff, I was about to broadcast on the world's largest Christian television network and be drawn more deeply into my destiny. All of this was thrust upon me without me ever inquiring about a television show or passing a business card to anyone. You have a purpose and a destiny.

Maybe your destiny is being birthed through a failed business or bankruptcy. Perhaps the downsizing of a company was really meant to shake you free to a life of purpose. It is not always the best or joyous moments that direct us to Destiny. Sometimes deep pain and torturous emotions later help to maneuver, mold, and position you into your life's purpose.

The overarching pull of Destiny helps you accept events and circumstances that, examined in isolation, may look like failure. Upon deeper reflection, however, those seeming tragedies are the catalysts that shift you into your place of destiny. The Bible rightly says in Romans 8:28, "And we know that God causes everything to work together for the good of those who love God and are called according to his purpose for them." The things that are working together may not feel good. They may not even seem fair. But if you allow them to, they can usher you into arenas and opportunities that shift your life into a pattern of focus and purpose that work together for your good and the good of humanity. Perhaps we all can lessen Destiny's learning curve and say, like Mrs. King so eloquently stated, "I was called to play this role in life!"

Find the destiny your Creator has designed for you. Have the courage to live with a consummate decision to say yes to what Destiny invites you to. Instincts are the internal guidance system that will empower you, and Destiny is the course that you will run, ignoring distractions that could divert you. Destiny gently pulls us through wandering mediocrity.

It is the destiny of this preacher from the hills of West Virginia to help you discover your destiny. Reflect on your own life. If you have ever sensed the pull of Destiny aligning you with people, places, and things, I will help you find your way.

CHAPTER 2

There *Is* More

Step toward Greater Fulfillment and Purpose

You feel it in every fiber of your being. You imagine it. You dream about it. You yearn for it. You fantasize about it. Deep in your gut you know there is more you can get out of life, and that knowledge gnaws at your insides, brewing a lingering unrest. You try to brush the feeling away, but it returns time and again. You may not know what your more is, but the desire is there. You keep reaching out for it, even if you don't know what you're grasping to attain. All you know is that you're not there yet.

"Maybe I'm being ungrateful or immature or unrealistic to want more. I've done well. I've been blessed. I should be content with what I have already achieved." Have you ever tried to suppress your longing for more with such words? Even as you console yourself with gratitude for what you have, you may not be able to shake a deep yearning for more. You can be the most grateful person in the world, but if you have not arrived at the place God wants you to be, to do the thing God has destined you and only you to do, that longing will never go away.

The fact that you yearn for more doesn't mean you're ungrateful for what you have or that you're greedy. It means you have a higher calling. The yearning inside calls you.

Your feelings of longing indicate that your present reality is too confining, maybe even suffocating, because you know there's more beyond what you now do, more beyond what you now know, more beyond what you now possess, and more beyond what you have experienced in life thus far. It doesn't matter whether your life is in the pits or you've reached the pinnacle of success in your career or community. You may not know where the search for more will lead, but a part of you longs to go after it—whatever *it* may be.

An inestimable number of people have asked, "Is this all there is to life?" The answer always lies within the very one who asks the question. If you determine in your mind to seek more, you will always find there's more you can get out of life. There's a greater impact you can have. There's a bigger footprint you can make during your short time on earth. Without even knowing your circumstances, I can tell you with certainty that the answer is, "Yes, there is more!"

What Does More Look Like?

Knowing what more looks like in your life is essential because you have to pursue the authentic more that is calling to you rather than a life expansion that is merely a diversion. Here's why it's vitally important to know what your more is. James is fifty-one years old and has held a steady, secure job for twenty-five years. It provides amply for his family. There's just one problem—he feels no fulfillment from his work because he's not challenged. But James believes that a middle-aged man cannot afford to quit a secure, well-paying job. So he gets up day after day, dresses, kisses his wife good-bye, and goes to spend another day at an unfulfilling but well-paying job. James longs to add something to his life that will restore a sense of purpose, but he believes his present circumstances determine the rest of his life. His practical mind is telling him life may offer him nothing more than a stable marriage and a secure job that provides a nice home for his family.

James doesn't know what his authentic more looks like as he strikes up a friendship with a new employee at the office. Carmen is eager to learn the ropes, and James has been there long enough to know them all. He is intrigued by her enthusiasm for her work and her drive to succeed. He's impressed with Carmen's desire to make a better life for herself and her children. Within a few months, their friendship veers to an intimate relationship that threatens James's marriage and both their jobs.

James's unguided search for more thrust him into an extramarital relationship when what he really longed for was to feel needed. His authentic more might have come from teaching a class or learning a new skill for personal enhancement. He may have invented a device to revolutionize the industry in which he works. James didn't pursue his authentic more with intentionality; rather, he slipped into a destructive diversion that only appeared to have something to offer.

More Beyond What You Can See Right Now

Before Italian explorer Christopher Columbus set sail from Spain in 1492 and stumbled upon the Americas, the Spaniards had prided themselves on their misinformed belief that their country was the last westward point of solid land on a flat earth. Early Spanish coins were inscribed with the words *ne plus ultra*—which is a Latin phrase meaning "no more beyond." They believed there was nowhere else to go after Spain, and if one ventured into the endless sea, certain danger lay ahead.

These same words, *ne plus ultra*, also have been stamped on the minds of many men and women who have great potential but who have not ventured past the limits of their self-imposed boundaries. They live in frustration because they believe there is no more beyond their current job, beyond their current state of physical health, beyond living from paycheck to paycheck, beyond having an unfulfilling marriage, or beyond living single. And even when they know there is more than what they are accustomed to, they may be paralyzed by the fear of what lies ahead if they try to pursue more.

The paralysis that confines us to living in small spaces is often rooted in fear fueled by the people closest to us. The people we love are sometimes guilty of encouraging us to live in *ne plus ultra* mode. A husband may be apprehensive about his wife's desire to go back to college and complete her degree. A best buddy may be intimidated by his friend's newfound interest in church or a more spiritual existence. A parent may be unsettled by a child's desire to move to a different city or a different country.

When you share your dreams with people who cannot envision more, their fearful comments can be discouraging. When people encourage you to live a life that yields less than what you're capable of accomplishing, there's usually a selfish motive. When the people closest to you try to confine your life to a small space, it's typically not because they're bad people or because they want you to feel like a failure. Most often they fear you will outgrow them and have no room for them in your life.

The problem of living in *ne plus ultra* mode is that our human nature compels us to seek more. No matter how much you say, "This is it," your spirit is telling you, "Keep searching." The life we are destined to live calls to us, and our spirits turn toward it. I hope you will heed the call to live in the larger space your spirit calls you into.

Discover *Plus Ultra* Living

The belief that there is nothing beyond what we can see or comprehend has been a great fallacy in human thinking throughout history. There is always more beyond. The Spaniards thought there was no land beyond their western border, but upon Columbus's return from the New World, they were compelled to make a rather embarrassing acknowledgment that indeed there is more beyond.

Legend says Alexander the Great was moved to tears because he believed there were no more worlds for him to conquer. In life, there are always more worlds to conquer. You may be a company CEO who is disenchanted with your success because you've forgotten how to be a whole person. All you talk about is work. Your *plus ultra* may be improving your marriage, getting in shape, or spending time with your grandchildren.

To move beyond mediocrity or the frustration of a life that's too small, align with God's purpose for your life. You were born for a distinct purpose, even if you have not yet figured out what that purpose is.

To find your life's *plus ultra* and fulfill your destiny, properly align with God's order for your life. The Supreme Architect put every facet of you together to accomplish what you alone were meant to contribute to the world.

What is your *plus ultra*? What is the more you want? It's called Destiny.

You Can't Win Just Playing Offense

People who are tuned in to the fact that they have Destiny and purpose are not malicious in their pursuit. Each of us has a divinely appointed destiny, and we don't have to fight offensively to attain it. Along your journey to Destiny, you will face challenges and struggles, but people don't experience true success in life by going on the offensive to fight their way ahead. Championship football teams have effective offensive and defensive players. They require a balance, depending on the strengths of the other team.

You will fight defensively against circumstances that can discourage or defeat you. You may duke it out with situations that threaten to bring you down. But if you are determined, you will not be defeated. It's not easy living your life aimed at Destiny.

I've had to do some fighting. I've fought my way against the odds. I fought to get to work despite hindrances like not having gas money or having a broken-down vehicle. I've fought to keep standing up when life tried to bring me down. I've fought to love and be loved. I've fought to get out of bed in the morning some days when it seemed like I couldn't endure my present circumstances. I've fought to live when circumstances predicted I should die. I've fought my doubts and my fears. I've fought my insecurities. I've fought haters and instigators, liars and betrayers. I've fought with family. There have even been times when I lay in bed, unable to sleep because I was fighting with myself! I've fought a good fight.

You engage in a good fight when you must beat the odds because you are determined to live in Destiny.

The person who quits after a setback is not Destiny-bound. These people are afraid, so they pass up opportunities. They don't want to get knocked down again, so they back down.

Maybe you always wanted to be a veterinarian but flunked Biology 101. Maybe you've always wanted a catering business but your first client ended up taking you to small claims court. There will always be challenges and setbacks, and no one is immune to a slip and fall on the journey to Destiny. Get back up and try again! Don't settle for the least out of life because you think you're not strong enough to get back up and try again.

Albert Einstein, the twentieth-century theoretical physicist, endured some setbacks. His parents were concerned that he was mentally challenged during his developmental years. When he applied for early admission into the Swiss Federal Polytechnical School, he failed everything except the math and science sections of the test. Einstein had to go to a trade school for a year before he was eligible to take the exam again and be admitted to school. If the man who remains the present-day standard of genius had intellectual and educational setbacks and got back up, why can't you?

When Radio One CEO Cathy Hughes and her husband divorced, she bought his share of the radio station they had purchased. Times got hard for Hughes, and for a while she was forced to give up her apartment and live at the station office to make ends meet. But she kept at it. Today, her company is the largest black-owned radio chain in America. Radio One also owns a successful cable channel. Hughes is the first African American woman to head a firm that is publicly traded on a stock exchange in the United States.

People like Einstein and Hughes succeed because they refuse to let lost battles push them out of their pursuit of Destiny. Success comes to those who get back up again and again because they are determined and unstoppable. They get back up and enroll for another semester, even after an academic setback. They get back up after a marital challenge and go to counseling to work out their issues. They get back up after a bankruptcy and get their finances in order. They get back up after a miscarriage and conceive again, adopt, or find other fulfillment for their parental instincts. They get back up after a prison sentence and find a legitimate means of pursuing their quality of life. They get back up after a broken trust and still believe in the goodness of humanity.

Destiny is a journey, and you will fall down a few times, and maybe even more. The key that opens the door to Destiny is your willingness to get back up after delay, disappointment, or even disaster.

They say that the mighty oak tree, which can grow up to eighty feet tall and a hundred feet wide, is nothing but a nut that refused to give up its ground. The acorn, which rarely gets larger than two inches tall, has the capacity to grow to nearly a thousand times its size! How tall can you grow? People who are determined to pursue Destiny sometimes look crazy to other people. You may look like an absolute nut to other people because you are unwilling to quit. They say, "You're going to try again? Even after what happened before?" Yes, even after what happened before, and before that, and before that! You can't let other people determine how far you are willing to go to reach Destiny because it's simply not their call. They don't get it, so don't worry about them!

Be the nut who won't give up ground, because every day teaches you something. Every day is a teacher that brings you new skills, new experiences, and new exposure. Get back up, because there is much to learn in pursuit of Destiny. The drive to get up and try again gives you experience and teaches you skills that will help you reach your destiny. You have to be equipped with the skills and expertise necessary to position you toward your destiny.

Sometimes the skills you gain in your pursuit of Destiny have more to do with building character and internal fortitude than with a particular skill set. You may learn the patience and attention to detail needed to run a specialty company while working in a menial entry-level job. I know from personal experience that nothing you have been through will be wasted. All you have been exposed to and all that you have experienced are in the repository that builds your future. You never know what tidbit of information or seemingly insignificant experience will become the bedrock of your destiny.

Get Inspired by People Who Help You Spiral Up

Think about how many devices have been created in the last hundred years versus the previous thousand years. Think about how many inventions exist today that were not even conceived of when you were born. Their potential to be was always there, but someone had to envision it. Someone had to look into the piles and piles of sawdust lying around in sawmills and see the creation of particleboard or fire-starter logs. Johannes Gutenberg had to see a machine that could print pages of text en masse and invent the printing press.

Your journey to your vision is no different. God created you with the raw materials you need to reach your destiny. What may be lacking in your life is a blueprint or design to pull together the raw materials inside you in the masterpiece of your life. Whenever you're tempted to think of yourself as incapable or inadequate, remember that the ingredients you need are already inside you.

Have you ever noticed that inventions seem to feed off each other? As a new gadget is invented, someone is inspired by that invention to create something more. Today, almost everyone has an electronic tablet or a smartphone—from grammar school students to grandmas. These powerful personal electronic devices were unthinkable just two decades ago. In the 1990s, we were still fascinated with laptop computers, which were inspired by the popularity and growing demand for personal computers. Each later invention was inspired by a previous one, each new invention expanding in capacity and capability from its predecessor. In the same way, people can be inspired by other people to do more and be more. Greatness inspires greatness. Creativity inspires creativity. When you align yourself with people who inspire you and help draw out the best in you, you find your best self.

We read the words of those who inspire us. We watch their lives and model their behavior. But let's not be misguided into thinking that they give us the power to produce. Oh, no, they do not! Some think that emulating those we admire makes us more effective and guarantees the result they exhibit. The goal is not to duplicate someone else's greatness or purpose, destiny or creativity.

We want to be successful at being uniquely original. Isn't that a liberating idea? Just think: the freedom to be in competition only with your own gifts and abilities. Too many people measure themselves by someone else's destiny. Consequently, they lead miserable existences, constantly ashamed that what others do requires them to reinvent themselves in order to compete. If you ascribe to your uniqueness, you will build alliances with those who can help unearth your treasure and avoid the perpetual failure of attempting to be someone or something that you are truly not!

The most those who inspire us can do is cause what is inherently within us to spiral up. That is the definition of inspiration in its purest form. It causes what's within to spiral upward. It is important that we have sources that inspire us as we inspire others. As we fill others with hope and encouragement, we need those who cause us to spiral upward as well. Remember, no matter how productive our lives have been, there is always something higher to reach toward. Inspiration is critical to Destiny. You will benefit greatly from associating with other people who have a vision for their lives and want to pursue that vision.

Imbalances in Our Lives Can Create Frustration

Life is about balance. We have joy and sorrow. Inevitably there are highs and lows. As we give to others and help them enhance their lives, we must not neglect to feed ourselves. As flight attendants tell us, we must first put our own mask on before attempting to help someone else. Sometimes we are the one needing to put a mask on someone else. At other times, we may need someone to put the mask on us. How frustrating would it be to sit on an airplane that has lost cabin pressure and have no oxygen mask? You have helped a half dozen people get their masks on, and now you need help but there's no one. You need someone to put your mask on for you, but if no is willing to help, what can you do? You would be extremely frustrated watching everyone else calmly seated, breathing while you gasp for air because no one helped you.

Think about how you feel when you're constantly giving. For a while, you feel rewarded because you have the joy of helping someone else. But after a while, you get back in tune with your own needs. "What about me?" you may ask. As you give and give of yourself, it's important to refuel by spending time with people who can pour into you. If you're always the giver and someone else is always the receiver, you're bound to become frustrated. Conversely, if you're always the receiver, you're still bound to be frustrated because there is no balance in the relationship. The best associations are those that provide balance through sharing. Just like in a marriage, sometimes you are the one who encourages, while at other times you are the one who needs to be encouraged, believed in, and lauded with honor.

Look at the areas of your life that cause you frustration. Discover the inequity that lies within and determine whether you can do something to resolve it. If it's your finances, figure out how to achieve balance through greater income or fewer expenditures. If you're dissatisfied in your relationships, look for areas of inequity to determine whether the relationships can be improved or whether they are terminally unequal. When you make a conscious decision to have balance in your life, you systematically eliminate the potential for frustration and misery.

Use What You Have to Help You Soar

Eagles have extremely powerful eyesight. Some species have vision that is almost four times human acuity. They can spot their potential prey from a great distance. The eagle sees an opportunity to grasp what he desires long before others can because of his vision. Once the eagle spots his prey, he goes after it.

Eagles also know how to use what are called thermals, which are rising currents of warm air, and updrafts to help them soar and to conserve their energy while soaring. When eagles fly long distances, they position themselves high in a thermal and then glide downward to catch the next thermal, where the process repeats.

Take a lesson from the majestic eagle's flight habits. Use what God has already placed around you to help you soar, like eagles use those warm currents of air. Then position yourself to take flight. Use that unfulfilling job to gain as much skill and expertise as you can to soar in a new environment one day. The proficiencies you gain while serving on that job you don't like may be just what you need to propel you to the next level. Standing on your feet all day as a salesclerk may develop in you the customer service skills needed to manage the day spa you will own one day. Your experiences as a security guard may inspire you toward a career in law enforcement. Work as a police officer may awaken a desire in you to earn a law degree and become a district attorney. Use what's available to you to soar higher!

You don't have to spend your life wondering what life might have been like if you had been willing to persevere to your dream. Destiny is already in your heart. You have seen it in your dreams or daydreams. You may have wondered, "Where did *that* come from?" Maybe what you imagined didn't come from you. Perhaps you were treated to a divinely planted glimpse into your future. Sometimes our dreams are so big that we can't possibly imagine they are for us. When I was growing up, older people in the church used to say, "God won't put more on you than you can bear." They most often used this expression to refer to troubled times. But the reverse is also true. God won't give you a vision or a destiny that is greater than what you can handle. Breathe in the vision that God has shown you and know that you can accomplish whatever the Creator has apportioned to you.

CHAPTER 3

Order Your Steps toward Destiny

Choose What's Important to You

Who wants steps? I don't like steps. Never have, even as a kid. When I was younger, I was impatient going up staircases, and because I have long legs, I would bound two or three steps at a time. I would find a way to maneuver around old people because I was too restless to wait for them to navigate their way up or down. I did that until the day I fell going up the steps. That fall taught me to respect steps. One at a time, they take you to the next level. Now that I'm older, I don't take on steps so hurriedly. I've learned that each step is important. When I was young, it was funny to me to see an older person take one step at a time, but now that I'm older, I've learned the race is not given to the swift.

Nobody wants steps. They're not attractive. We try to decorate them with fancy wood and railings, but the only reason we have steps is to get us to a higher level. If there was a way to get to a higher level without steps, we would take it.

The Bible says in Psalm 37:23 that the steps of a good man are ordered by the Lord. The word *steps* implies process. God orders steps. That means Destiny is going to take a while. *Steps* mean you can't get to the destination just because you want to, would like to, or even need to. You can stand on the first floor of a building and look up the staircase to the next floor for as long as you want, but all the wishing, hoping, and praying in the world are not going to get you to the second floor until you take the steps.

You're standing on the first floor of your life. Your first-floor life has all the basics, and you may be fine with that until you see a staircase to stories above and glimpse what you never imagined. That's Destiny, and you want to go up there. You want to be on one of those top floors. But you can't get up there quickly. You must take the steps.

You want to hasten the process to Destiny, get to an expected end, but that cannot be done. No shortcuts. No way to bypass some steps. No elevator to Destiny.

Steps do not make life harder; they create readiness. God knows that a blessing given too soon is not a blessing at all.

Suppose your twenty-year-old son needs transportation. You gift him keys to his own car—a blessing to him to get to school or work. But if you had given him his own car when he was ten, that wouldn't have been a blessing to him or to the others on the road. Ten years earlier, the same son given the same car may have yielded a tragic outcome because he couldn't have handled it then. Before getting the car, your son needed to go through the steps of driver education. He needed to study the manual for his learner's permit and prepare for the written test. He needed to take and pass the written test. He needed to practice driving on side streets and empty parking lots with an experienced driver in the passenger seat to help him. Then he needed to pass the road test and receive his license. He needed to demonstrate trustworthiness to you when he borrowed the family car and returned it when promised, no scratches, clean and gassed up. There are many steps before that ten-year-old boy is ready for the blessing a new car is to a twenty-year-old. Steps are part of our maturation. If we get what God has in store for us too soon, we can't handle it.

Respect Steps, Establish Order

Establishing order in your life is essential preparation for Destiny. Once you set your order, you will awaken each day determined to engage those principles to pursue your purpose. You will wake up focused because you have an agenda. When you wake up with a reason for being, you have the drive to get up and try all over again if necessary and not worry about what happened yesterday. Setbacks won't cause you to drop out of the game. Disappointments won't cause you to stay in bed with the covers pulled over your head. Your destiny is a daily call to get up and get back in the game.

When your life is ordered, setbacks and disappointments are regarded as commas and not periods that punctuate your life story. Each day is a new opportunity to live your dream when your life is ordered for Destiny. Maybe you haven't arrived there yet, but every step you take toward it is still living your dream. You're not the *New York Times* best-selling author yet, but writing for a local community paper is still living your dream as you gain the skills you need. You're not the owner of your own trendy clothing boutique yet, but the classes you're taking in fashion merchandising are steering you in the direction of Destiny. Day by day and step by step you stay on task, especially when times are tough. When we live in pursuit of Destiny, each step positions us closer and closer.

Don't look at how far away you are. Respect the journey you're on because it will take you higher if you stick with it. Respect the sacrifices you're making now because they will help you appreciate your accomplishments. You will look back over your hardships and respect, and yes, even admire the person you were along the journey. You can look back at the person who endured all the adversity life threw at you but kept moving forward, and encourage others to stay the course to Destiny. You will have confidence in yourself and contentment with life because you know you are in the place where you belong.

When I was young, my mother and father went into a very nice store in Charleston, West Virginia, called Goldfarb that sold light fixtures. My family was, as the young people say, "on the come up," and they were decorating a house we had just built. My mother had looked among all the finery exhibited and identified a very exquisite set of lamps that she adored. They were on sale at a great price and my mother really wanted the lamps. My father inquired about purchasing them only to find out that they were on hold for another customer. I saw disappointment glaze my mother's eyes and cascade down her jawline into a grimace. I assumed it was prudent either to leave or settle for something else. Instead, my father said, "I'll wait!"

I thought, "Wait for what?"

"If that customer doesn't return," he said, "I want them." He sat down in that store and waited all day! By five o'clock that evening, the customer hadn't returned and my father bought the lamps. As lovely as the lamps were, what illuminated my soul was what can happen if you are tenaciously in orderly pursuit of what you want.

Have Patience with the Process

I don't like process or anything that has drawn-out procedures. I don't like paperwork. I don't like waiting in line. I don't like those automated phone lines with voice prompts that tell me to press five and then press one and then press…Maybe I'm just spoiled because I'm the baby of my family. I just want things to happen. I never wanted God to order my steps. When I've petitioned God, I've wanted the Almighty to—presto!—send a blessing, healing, or opportunity. Yet every time, the Creator ordered steps. God didn't offer steps as an option. My Maker did not present me a variety of options to choose from. The Lord ordered steps.

As I've grown in my Destiny journey, I'm now thankful that God *ordered* steps. It lets me know I am not moving aimlessly, nor am I moving on my own. I recognize there is a course for me to take, a divinely orchestrated process. I can't graduate to the next level until I take the current course and finish it.

At times I've prayed for God to design the course my way. That didn't happen, and I'm glad. I've learned that God isn't just making this up as the Spirit goes. The Lord ordered steps. Many times I was impatient and prayed that God abort the process. Other times I prayed God would speed things up, put my life on fast-forward. I've prayed to get out of things God wanted me to stay in. God knew I needed the experience of the process. I've prayed that I wouldn't have to endure some things the Lord has let me endure. Wisdom allowed endurance to mold me. When I tried to rush the process, God slowed me down, as if saying, "No, you skipped that step. Go back." Every time I saw a destination, God saw *me* and ordered my circumstances to ready me for where I was trying to go.

Accept the process. Your blessing is already ready. It's already done. God is getting *you* ready for the blessing, preparing you for your destiny. The process must be undergone so you can handle what you will face when you get to where you want to go.

God has to guide you through a process to prepare you. You may want children but not be ready to parent. You may want a spouse but not be ready for marriage. You're asking God for more in your life, but you have to learn how to handle what you have.

"Hang in there!" is encouragement to keep pushing forward through stressful and trying times, but that's easier said than done. Patience is tough work. It's hard to keep pressing toward Destiny while everything around you seems to be falling apart. Difficult to keep loving that man you fell in love with twenty years ago while he's going through his midlife crisis. You didn't envision a husband with an earring and tattoos! But you take your vows seriously, so you hang in there. Or maybe you're challenged to get up every morning, go to work on time, dedicated and with a good attitude, when you know you're being set up for termination. When you took the job, you thought you would retire from that company. But you need your job, so you hang in there. Or maybe you feel the pain of watching the mother you thought was invincible endure the mental and physical deterioration of Alzheimer's. But now it's your turn to care for her, even though she doesn't recognize you most days, and you hang in there. You probably have experienced a time when nothing in your life looks like what you imagined, hoped for, prayed for, planned for, and strategized for. "Hang in there!" is frustrating to hear, but that's what you have to do.

Destiny means focusing on a vision, seeing what's not there yet. Don't let go of it. Your dream may be the only thing that excites you. And you may have to keep it to yourself. How dare you have a dream? Who are you to imagine for yourself a life that is more interesting, more purposeful, more challenging, or even more opulent? Don't get upset if no one understands: just hold tightly to your vision, because no matter who you are, you're not going to get there overnight. When it seems Destiny is slipping right through your fingers, tighten your imaginative grasp and declare, "It's mine and I'm not letting it get away, no matter what I have to go through!"

Many forfeit the hard work of process. They don't hang in there because life can be very, very hard. They get disenchanted with process because they don't see results. They fail to realize they have to grow and circumstances must evolve. They don't know that the oak tree they imagined is somewhere in the acorn they received.

Process precedes accomplishment. Have the tenacity to endure the process, because what you learn will help you survive when you attain your goal. If you learn to be patient, you will become consistent in your pursuit of Destiny.

Although the Bible says the Lord orders the steps of a good person, most of us are looking for the elevator! God doesn't promise elevators; the Lord guides steps. The steps strengthen us. So get on the StairMaster and stick with it!

I spent years pastoring a church with little growth. I often wondered if I had what it took to reach a broader audience. I didn't understand that while I was trying to build a church, God was trying to build a man! The only way to build the man was to put him in an environment that exercised his faith muscles and built up his experience. Otherwise, I wouldn't be able to handle success!

The order of service at Potter's House is very detailed, down to the minute. One pastor looked at our service schedule and said, "Services at my church are more spontaneous. There might be an impromptu solo or a testimony." I responded that the sheer number of worshippers at Potter's House necessitates a high level of organization. The more you manage, the more you must prepare. The more you desire, the more process is required. When you ask God for more, accept that more order will be required of you. If you're driving a fancy sports car or a new hybrid, you can make a quick, swift turn at the spur of the moment. But if you're driving an eighteen-wheeler, you have to prepare to make that turn.

Prioritize, Focus, Ignore

How do you bring the vision of your heart, mind, and spirit into reality to get to that place you were destined to be? You need order in your personal life. To live your goals, you must set priorities, focus on them, and learn to ignore tugs on your time, energy, and resources that are outside of Destiny's call.

I realized that if I was going to fulfill God's vision for my life and live out my destiny, I had to learn how to accept that our all-powerful God created in me a limited resource. I can only do so much in the course of a day or a season of my life. My various roles are husband, father, pastor, business owner, etc. I cannot give them all equal attention every day. I cannot meet the demands of each responsibility equally every day. I know that at the end of each day, one of those areas will come up lacking. Some days I'm a better business owner than a husband. Other days, I'm a better father than I am a pastor. What is important to me, however, is that I don't allow the same area of responsibility to go lacking every day. Every day I prioritize. Every day I live my destiny.

I have an order by which my life is structured. On any given day, I *prioritize*. I determine what is most important and what most needs my attention. After I have prioritized, I *focus*. I put my concentration and energy on the tasks and situations that I have determined most need my attention. Equally important to prioritizing and focusing is the ability to *ignore.* What someone else deems a crisis may not be my crisis, or it may not be a situation that merits my attention that day.

You may be missing tremendous opportunities because you have not ordered what it takes in your life to get ahead. It is so vitally important that your life has an order and a rhythm so you won't miss the seasons of life when you are most productive and vital. You can't sign up for more than you can deliver and you can't focus on any one responsibility for too long.

When my children were younger, they loved having me around the house. But I knew that if I spent too much time around the house, I would not be making money to support my family. My kids couldn't play their video games with no power because the electric bill hadn't been paid! They wouldn't have fun wrestling each other on the floor if their stomachs were growling. So sometimes they had to miss me a little so I could keep food on the table.

Since each of us has a destiny, it is important for each of us to have a personal strategy for accomplishing what we long to do in life. Each of us is unique. Each of us has a function and a purpose that no one else can fulfill. Establish your own personal priorities so that you live your authentic life.

Have you ever admired an actor in a movie or had a favorite recording artist who seemingly dropped off the scene? You may have even wondered why a person would give up a lifestyle of fame and adulation. Sometimes people become famous only to discover it's not the lifestyle that empowers them to fulfill their destiny. Some singers don't want the pressure of creating another hit record. They just want to make music. Some actors don't want to lose the ability to go grocery shopping without being mobbed by fans. They just want the opportunity to use their gifts. Sometimes people back away from fame or notoriety, but not because they didn't have the talent. Instead they come to realize that the pressures of pursuing fame do not fit into their destiny. Fame is not the highest expression of Destiny; neither is wealth. Most people live out their destiny without fortune or fame. Some have affected many, many lives, but became neither rich nor famous in fulfilling their destiny.

God has not designed one person to be better than another. Your destiny is yours. Own it and pursue it. It doesn't matter where you were born or your current education level—you can rise to where you were destined to be. Don't waste time comparing yourself or your destiny with someone else's.

You were created for a reason. You are alive for a reason. Pursue that reason with passion and live in your true purpose.

When you see others fulfilling their destiny, you may feel jealousy or envy. They've gotten to a place you haven't or believe you can't. Don't go there! You need all of your energy to work toward your own purpose, even if you haven't realized precisely what that is yet. Rejoice with those who are walking in their own Destiny. When feelings of jealousy seem to overpower you, remind yourself that you have a Destiny. Be thankful God has designed a purpose for you and that you are on your way to fulfilling what you were put on this earth to do. If you are tempted to feel envious, use those feelings to inspire you to emulate, not hate. Tell yourself, "If he can do it, so can I!" Think of how happy you will be for yourself and how happy you will want others to be for you as you climb your own ladder of success.

Think of your destiny and everyone else's in this way: Imagine you are running or walking on a track to improve your physical condition. It doesn't make sense to be jealous of the person running past you in the next lane. Maybe she's been training longer. Her level of fitness has no impact on your own, just as yours has no impact on the person in the other lane that you just passed. Instead of being jealous, compliment her. Find out how she optimized her physical condition, and set out to do the same, because jealousy is energy that is better spent on building up yourself.

God wants you to *prioritize*, *focus*, and *ignore* so you can reach the place you were meant to be. When you have your priorities in place, you can focus on them and give them the attention they deserve because you know what's important. When you know what's important, you can ignore the things that can only distract you from arriving at Destiny.

Acquire the Skill of Guiltless Prioritization

Destiny is a deliberate pursuit. To position yourself toward Destiny, you will, of necessity, have to understand that certain actions, behaviors, and relationships are essential, as opposed to things that are tangential. You can invest yourself in many good things that have nothing to do with arriving at your destiny. If you want to be a radiologist, you can become a hospital volunteer and do great work helping people, but volunteering won't help you pass MCATs, get you accepted into medical school, or help you make good grades once you get in.

You can associate with many good people, but if they are wandering aimlessly through life and encouraging you to "chill" and stop stressing about the future, you may want to rethink your associations. Your best friend from high school may be a distraction from Destiny. Your old buddy from the military may be a deterrent to Destiny. The crowd from your job that invites you to hang out with them after work may be interfering with Destiny. The boyfriend who demands all your time and wants you to have no outside interests may be standing in the way of Destiny.

The difficulty with setting priorities sometimes rests in the fact that most of us have been conditioned to help others and to not be selfish in life. People can sometimes try to make you feel guilty for saying no to them because what they want is not what you have prioritized. It's not selfish to prioritize your life to fulfill Destiny. It's actually the most selfless thing you can do. God has an appointment for you to serve humanity in the greatest way possible for you. Therefore, you owe it to yourself, to others, and to the Creator to prioritize your life in preparation for Destiny.

Life is full of distractions—some positive, some menacing—so prioritizing your life keeps you on track and simplifies the cutting-away process when circumstances or people attempt to divert you from your goal. Determine your priorities and write them down. Writing is a powerful tool because you can go back to what you've written and see if you're still on the right course. Some of life's distractions can't be helped. It's possible to become legitimately sidetracked when we are moving toward Destiny. Having a child can cause you to reprioritize, for a time, so that you can give care and attention to the baby. A parent or other loved one may become ill and need ongoing care. It's understandable that you will have to take care of a loved one, and no child or ill loved one should be made to feel guilty because of those circumstances.

Prioritizing your life means owning your vision for Destiny. It's yours and no one else's, so order your life to accomplish what you desire. Human beings must be in order to function as the effective, influential, capable creatures God created. As you take ownership of Destiny, you will become comfortable with determining the steps, actions, and people who support your vision. Not everyone is going to understand, so get over that. Mama and Daddy may not get it. Your twin brother may not get it. Your business partner may not get it. It's not their vision, so don't expect them to understand. God didn't give it to them, so they can't see what God has shown you. They don't feel excitement coursing through their veins when you talk about the vision. Frankly, they just don't get it. Some people can be downright discouraging. "What are you wasting your time with that for?" "Are you still fooling with that mess?" "Aren't you ready to give that up by now?"

Because they can't see your vision, people can get you off track, even if they don't directly express opposition to your vision. They don't mean to, but they just have other plans for your time and for your life. Your sister wants you to buy a time-share with her. Your wife thinks you should coach Little League. Your child's teacher is begging you to run for PTA president. Your fraternity brother wants you to set aside some money and accompany him to the next national convention. Other people have no problem putting demands on your time, but you don't have time for what's on their agenda because you are stretching yourself toward Destiny.

You can spend your time doing great things. That's what makes prioritizing essential. We can do great things to help other people, our community, our church, or even our family members, but prioritizing helps you recognize whether you can invest time and energy in such great deeds apart from your vision. Prioritization keeps you from allowing others to distract your attention from pursuing Destiny.

You will never reach your destination if you cannot stay focused on your true priorities. Does that mean you should fail to provide adequately for your family because you are pursuing your dream? Certainly not! Failing to support your family because you are consumed with the selfish pursuit of a dream is unconscionable. It doesn't mean you get a pass from keeping a roof over your children's heads. It does mean that for a while family vacations may be three-day road trips to a nearby amusement park instead of a week in Hawaii.

I've seen people become intellectually, emotionally, spiritually, financially, or professionally near death. They live and work on life support. They exist rather than live. Yes, they have some happy moments, but these are few. Have you ever spent time around a terminally ill person? As the person transitions to eternity, she experiences brief moments of awareness and brief moments of joy. She does not have the energy to engage life.

I know people who are alive but have no life in them. The light of life has gone out or never even been kindled because they failed to prioritize and missed opportunities. When you see people miss opportunities, it helps you understand the importance of establishing priorities. Vocalists who are serious about a singing career know they have to pursue it while they're young because rarely do record companies sign artists over age thirty. If singers miss that opportunity during their youth, they may never get it again. That's not to say other opportunities won't come, but no matter how many chances people get, if they have not prioritized their lives for Destiny, they will simply keep missing out on possibilities.

Are You Living Evidence of an Ordered Life?

Growing up I would often hear folks in church say, "God does things decently and in order." I didn't really know what it meant back then, but I do now. God's purpose for your life cannot manifest in the midst of chaos. You can't reach the place you were destined to be if you're constantly getting sidetracked. You cannot reach your life purpose when everything in your life is undisciplined, distracted, and disordered.

One dictionary definition for *disorderly* is "messy." Have you ever felt like your life is a mess? Your life is not a mess because of situations beyond your control. Your life is a mess because you have failed to prioritize the handling of those situations. When you prioritize the important things in your life, people who are not good for you do not receive your attention. All your time is needed for your priorities. The friend who's encouraging you to cheat on your husband will get cut loose when your marriage is a priority. So will the buddy who thinks life is all about being a slacker, when Destiny is your priority. The boss who threatens to fire you if you don't lie in your report will be part of your past when your integrity is a priority. Habits that hinder you from Destiny get overcome: the drug abuse, the shopping addiction, the gossiping habit. What will not support your journey to Destiny gets cut loose, unapologetically. If you feel guilty about setting your priorities and cutting loose hindrances, you may not make it to Destiny.

I've seen talented people fail to reach their full potential because they cannot set priorities. They are afraid of hurting someone's feelings. They don't want anyone to be mad at them. They want to be accepted by people who don't even matter. They are afraid to make Destiny more important than peer pressure.

A few years ago, a number of news and magazine shows told the story of Ted Williams, dubbed "the homeless man with the golden voice." Ted was blessed with a speaking voice sent from heaven. After taking off on a promising career in radio, Ted's priorities got skewed. He got sidetracked by drugs and alcohol. After years of homelessness and addiction, a Columbus, Ohio, videographer filmed Ted and his golden voice begging on the streets. The video went viral and Ted was inundated with offers for voice-over work in television, in radio, and on the Internet. People were donating to a special website created for him because they didn't want to see his great talent go to waste. Always remember, people love to get behind a winner. Even in this age of skepticism and mistrust, people are still willing to give, to support, and to provide a leg up to people to see them be the best they can be.

Ted's melodious voice and natural talent were not enough to steer him toward the place he longed to be as a young college student. Somehow, he aligned himself with activities and people and situations that shifted his promising career downward. His talent was not enough to save him from a lack of priorities and the poor choices that resulted.

When your life is not in order, you feel discomfort. A little piece of lint in your eye can give you unbelievable pain. A few grains of sand stuck down in your carburetor can jam up the entire engine. When you conduct your life haphazardly, without prioritization, you have dis-ease caused by unimportant things taking the place of what is important to your destiny.

Ordering Your Life Takes Time

God's plan for your life is so awesome, so amazing, that you have to get it in stages. The Almighty can't show it all to you right away. It might scare you, so you get it in pieces to digest a bit at a time. As you are digesting, settle your affairs in order to receive the full revelation of Destiny. These things take time. Now is the time to order your life and set your priorities straight. So as Destiny is unfolding, use that time to order your life and you'll be ready to receive the life that is waiting for you. Just as a mother eagle gives her growing eaglets time to learn how to flex their wings and navigate the winds that will carry them, God gives you time to learn and to grow.

Any life transition requires time. There's a reason people hire personal trainers. When you become serious about getting or staying physically fit, you recognize that you need a plan. When you walk into a health club, you need a plan so that all your body's muscles are developed. A personal trainer helps you establish an order for your workout, according to the health goals you have set and the results you want to achieve. Once you have a plan in place, getting to the level of physical fitness you want will take time. Then a trainer will help you stay on track if you're tempted to get off.

Setting your priorities becomes like having a personal trainer. Priorities guide you to stay on course to Destiny. Then you order your life around those priorities. An ordered life is in tune with the rhythm of life. When your life is in order you are more likely to pay attention to subtle changes that may be signaling a major shift or movement in your life. When your life is chaotic, there may be major changes going on around you, but you miss them because you can't focus on what's going on right before you.

Your life may be in total chaos right now, but that just means now is a good time to start setting some priorities. You can't change everything at the same time and you can't change everything quickly. Just start with one area of your life. You may want to start by setting a budget, or maybe just a budget for one aspect of your finances. Start an exercise program. Cut a couple of credit cards in half. Read a book to improve your skills in the field you want to pursue. The key is to start. Ordering your life doesn't happen by magic. There's no hocus pocus, just sheer dedication to staying on task on a daily basis.

Human beings function best when there is structure in our lives, but it often takes time to get your life in order. It takes time to get enough sense and maturity to figure out who you are and who you are not. It takes time to figure out what you need to focus on or what you need to put your energy into. It takes time to recognize what is essential and what is trivial.

When I learned that being unfocused only served to move me away from my greater purpose, I figured out ways to keep order in my life. Look at every relationship, every task, every association, every financial investment, and every time investment to determine whether they will serve your journey to

Destiny. Then be prepared to cut away the things that are not beneficial to your progress. The cutting-away process may be difficult, but think of it as a life-and-death decision. You might find that when you prioritize, you won't need to do much cutting because people at the bottom of your list will often cut you off. Choosing to cut away associations and actions that don't deserve your focus means giving life to Destiny. Hanging on to situations, behaviors, and people that are not your priorities can only block your route to Destiny.

You get to decide. Will you bring life to your dream or will you allow it to die of neglect? It is absolutely true that you have a divine summons to fulfill, but it's not automatic and it's not guaranteed. You are the major player who must give yourself fully to the process of becoming.

Understand the power of making sound decisions, not quick ones. I once heard a motivational speaker advise his audience, "When you don't know what to do, just do something." As I listened, I thought it was the most misguided piece of advice I had ever heard. You can't just do something and hope it works, because it just may affect the next twenty years of your life. You can't just up and decide to get married or move to a new city or buy a new house based on quick or impulse thinking and expect to have the best outcome.

You might have told yourself, "Well, it's time for me to get married. I'm thirty-two years old." So you marry Willie. But for the next twenty years, you're mad and miserable. You're angry with Willie and sniping at him all the time. But you're not really angry with Willie. You're angry with yourself for making an impulse decision that has affected your life, Willie's life, and the lives of any children you may have had. Willie might have been someone else's dream man, but instead he's become your nightmare because you married him without thinking it through. Ordering your life with Destiny decisions takes time.

It's Never a Convenient Time

Eaglets never sense that it's time to leave the nest and move on to their destiny. But their parents know when it's time. The mother eagle begins to take away the leaves and padding she so dutifully placed in the nest in preparation for their birth. She watches them as they hatch and grow. Left to its own devices, an eaglet might never leave the nest, instead remaining content to let Mom keep bringing food. But the mother knows when the time is near. The process of eagles learning to fly is not nearly as detached as some may think. While the eaglet learns to take steps and flap its wings in preparation for that first flight, the parents are rarely far away. They may even watch as their eaglets practice flapping their wings and testing the branch on which they are perched. The eaglets are getting ready while their parents watch.

Like the eagles, God does not thrust you out of your comfort zone and turn away. Even as you test your strength and try to navigate your way to where you have never been, God is still near, watching so you will not fall.

Maybe you feel it's not time for change in your life. It may not seem like a good time to shift your priorities or start reordering life plans. It may not be the right time to change jobs, to go back to school, to move to a new city, to break away from an unhealthy relationship, or to change your spending habits. That's when God begins stirring the nest, initiating disruption so you will get moving.

Think about the major changes that have come into your life. Did any of them happen at a convenient time? When you understand that your timing and God's timing are different, you are in a better position to accept life's inconveniences. Bankruptcy may be the ordering you need to establish sound financial planning for your future. The timing for events that happen in your life may seem bad for what you understand right now. You may lose your job two weeks before Christmas, and it may seem like the worst kind of timing, but the timing can be totally relevant to Destiny. A present inconvenience may be necessary for a long-term benefit.

The time to shift your priorities in the direction of Destiny is never convenient. There will always be a reason to put it off until later. There will always be someone who gets angry with you for prioritizing your life in a way that affects what he or she wants you to do. Maybe your cousin will stop speaking to you because you can no longer babysit, but that's no reason to put off enrolling in night classes. Your children may be angry with you for putting the family on a budget, but you can't put off saving for their college education because of that. Your sister may stop speaking to you because you won't pay her rent anymore, but it may be time for you to stop making her rent more of a priority than securing your own financial future. Maybe someone you considered a friend will kick you to the curb because you stop hanging out so much with the fellas to be with your girlfriend. Prioritize your relationships and you will discover who your real friends are.

You will always find excuses to wait. Your decision to prioritize Destiny will always make someone angry, but better that person be angry with you than for you to be angry with you. I guarantee you will end up an angry person the day you awaken spiritually and realize that you've adhered to everyone's priorities except your own. Your chief priority is an appointment with Destiny!

CHAPTER 4

Destiny Is Spelled P-R-I-O-R-I-T-I-Z-E

Get Your Relationships, Money, and Thoughts in Step with Your Destiny

When you understand the steps needed to take you to the next level, the only way you can feel content about your life is if you are living according to the priorities you have set. Other people may not understand your choices or your lifestyle, and may even ridicule you for them, but when you know why you are making certain choices, their criticism doesn't matter. The haters don't matter. Your happiness will come from setting the priorities you need for the vision you have locked into.

That doesn't mean you won't have frustrating moments. That doesn't mean you won't want to give up sometimes. It means that when your life is prioritized in a way that makes sense for you to reach Destiny, you experience definite satisfaction and true contentment.

While other people are seeking satisfaction through things

or people or social standing, you have an opportunity for true joy and contentment by having your priorities in order. Your priorities are right when you make choices that lead you toward Destiny. So what if your cell phone still flips open and doesn't have a touch screen? So what if date night consists of a frozen pizza and a two-dollar DVD from a vending machine? So what if the bottoms of your shoes are not red and you don't have a handbag with someone's name on it? So what if you don't wear a suit and tie to work? So what if you pass up a date to stay home to help your child with his algebra? So what if you pull away from visionless people who have no plans for their future and don't want you to have any, either? When you make decisions about what is best for you based on your priorities, you are much less likely to be concerned about critical commentary from people who have nothing to do with your destiny.

Prioritize Your Relationships

I spoke in Ghana to a group of CEOs, politicians, and faith leaders about the importance of relationships. Anyone who understands business knows that the ability to build and maintain relationships with clients, customers, staff, and other companies is a prerequisite for successful business. If you can't build relationships, you are being torn down. Building relationships takes time that people often aren't willing to devote, partly because time is a limited resource for us all. Most of us have, at one time or another, spent a lot of energy, time, and effort investing in relationships that show little return. I don't necessarily mean financial return. I mean advancement, growth, or alignment with your vision. I'd rather you waste my money than waste my time. I earnestly believe that you must quantify the time you spend in relationships that may not be destructive but yet may be counterproductive to what you are trying to accomplish. It's not enough to invest money into your destiny if you waste time.

The true barometer to help you evaluate the relationships to invest in must center on this significant question: How does this person fit into my destiny and purpose? If you would approach your time with the same sense of fiduciary duty as your money, you would see a far greater return. People who are truly engaged want to know, "Where do I fit in your life and destiny?" Until that question can be answered, good people will leave you because they can't live in the clutter of your indecisiveness! To maximize the years you have left, clear the clutter!

Priorities can require us to find new friends and associates. Be selective and determine your associations carefully. Prioritize the persons with whom you will spend time and know why they are in your life. Your old buddy from junior high may not be the best person for you to associate with. You may be from the "hood" and try to prove that you haven't forgotten where you came from. Old acquaintances may even accuse you of forgetting where you came from. Staying in touch with the old gang from the "hood" is not a requirement for Destiny, and you don't have to prove yourself to anyone. Sometimes you simply have to break away from unhealthy people and relationships. When ex-offenders are placed on parole or probation, very often there are stipulations regarding persons they may spend time with to reduce the likelihood of a repeat offense.

The first thing to do in deciding what stays in your life and what goes is to determine what nourishes you and strengthens you. While it is nice to be philanthropic, many are trying to help while they are not capable of standing strong themselves. If you've been off track and lost time, missed moments, and had failures and delays, before you can help from your heart, you have to stabilize your head. Making decisions that invest before you make decisions that withdraw is critical for survival, whether in finances or relationships or time management. Ultimately, we want to be successful so that we can make a difference in the lives of others. But before you can be successful, you have to be a survivor.

To move from survival to success, we must begin by investing in what invests in us. Pour into relationships that pour into you. I know that sounds like common sense, but it is not that common. You've got to have somebody who can feed you so you can feed somebody else. Many people feed others who can't feed them, while they completely fail to nourish those who really desire to feed them. When Deuteronomy 25:4 says, "Don't muzzle the mouth of the ox that treads the grain," it simply means feed what is feeding you! If you're feeding people who can't feed you, it's only a matter of time before that constant feeding will begin to drain you. Don't keep feeding the same people for years and years. Be intentional about the people you are connected to.

If you are to live as a child of Destiny, you will interact with three basic types of people.

The first and most important type of person you will encounter is a confidant. You will have very few of them in your lifetime. In fact, if you find two or three in your entire lifetime, you are tremendously blessed. Confidants are the people who love you unconditionally. They are into you. They have your back whether you're up or down. They are with you for the long haul. If you get in trouble, they won't abandon you. Confidants will come get you out of jail. They'll pull you out of a drug house and love you all the while. You need a good confidant in order to reach Destiny.

Confidants are for you and with you and intimately intertwined in your life. They are with you to make sure you reach Destiny. They will challenge you and confront you to stay on the path to Destiny. They will get all in your business and in your face if they think you are out of order. They are not afraid to tell you when you're wrong and affirm you when you are right. Without them you'll never be who God called you to be.

The next type of person you will encounter is constituents. You will likely have many of them in your lifetime. Constituents are not into you; rather, they are into what you are for. They are not for *you*, nor does your destiny matter to them. But as long as you are for what they are for, they will walk with you and work with you. But it ends there. Never think they are on your team to stay for the long haul. Constituents are not confidants. Understand the nature of constituents because these are the people who will walk away if they meet someone else who will further their agenda.

Constituents are always looking for a better deal. They will abandon you to hook up with another person who better serves their purpose or their need. But if you understand who constituents are and their role and purpose in your life, you won't be too sad when they walk away. They were never in your life for you; they were in your life because they perceived that you and they were for the same thing. They were with you as long as you were for what they were for.

Throughout your life, it's essential not to get caught up in the hype of a constituency. Any politician can tell you that. Have you ever seen a popular politician fall from the grace of his or her constituents? It's amazing to watch as the transgressions of a beloved political figure come to light. Suddenly and swiftly, those who once were supporters begin to back away. Take care not to mistake your constituents for your confidants, particularly at times when you are broken. Constituents will fool you because after you've fallen in love with them, they will break your heart as they abandon you to connect with someone else who is for what they are for.

The last people group you will encounter is comrades. They are not for you, nor are they for what you are for. They are against what you are against. Comrades make strange bedfellows. They will team up with you, not so you can reach your destiny, but to fight a common enemy. Don't be fooled or confused by the close connection. They will only be with you until the victory happens. Comrades are like scaffolding. They come into your life to fulfill a purpose. They give you support for a time, but that time will only last as long as the common enemy lasts. When the purpose is complete, the scaffolding is removed. But don't be upset when the scaffolding is taken away, because the building is still standing.

Prioritize your associations with confidants, constituents, and comrades. Expect the constituents and the comrades to leave you after a while. And please don't be upset when they don't react to your dream the way you expected them to, because they were never for you or with you in the first place. By now you may be thinking that it would simply be easier to avoid both constituents and comrades alike, but that's not how the world operates. The only thing you need to do is be careful and prioritize your relationships knowing the position and role people play in your life. For instance, be careful whom you tell your dream to, because if you tell your dream to your constituents, they will desert you and try to fulfill the dream without you. If you tell comrades, they won't support you because they were never for what you were for anyway. Seek the people in your life who are safe to share your dream with. And if you find just a few during your lifetime, you are indeed blessed.

If you are dating a young lady who berates you for not having the material things you've delayed purchasing to fulfill your dream, she may be just a constituent. If your neighbor has never treated you kindly but comes to you because he wants your help to defeat an amendment that will negatively affect your neighborhood, don't get too excited. He's probably just a comrade. When the bill gets defeated, after the election, he will go right back to ignoring you.

You can separate your comrades and constituents from someone who has the potential to be a confidant with a simple test. If someone is really with you they will weep when you weep and they will rejoice when you rejoice. If you share some good news with someone and they don't rejoice with you, stop telling them your business! Try it sometime: If you walk into a room and tell someone about good things that are happening to you, stop celebrating long enough to watch their reaction. If they are not happy for you, shut your mouth, turn around, and walk back out the door. Share your dream with people who want you to succeed.

Prioritize Your Finances

The journey to Destiny includes every part of your life, especially your finances. Financial advisors will tell you they can look at your bank statement and know where your priorities lie. What does your bank account say about you? Do you look like a million dollars with only a few dollars in the bank and nothing saved for retirement? Are you barely making minimum payments on your credit cards? Are all of your credit cards at their maximum balance?

Financial advisors have a saying that if you are sitting on your assets, your priorities are all wrong. In other words, if all of your discretionary income is spent on expensive clothes or cars or handbags and you have no money saved for a rainy day or retirement, your priorities are misplaced. Prioritize your spending so that all of your money is not blown on things that depreciate. Think about the mobile phone you have. If you have one of the latest smartphones, you probably paid a premium price for it. How much is it worth now? Technology changes quickly, so the phone you paid $350 for a year ago is only worth $150 now.

Look at how you spend your money. Are you obsessed with the latest electronic gadgets? Can you drive a car for years after it's paid for? Can you wear clothes that don't come from certain stores? There's nothing wrong with shopping for quality, but the clothes you wear and the car you drive can never make you great. Destiny has nothing to do with impressing other people with the things you own. You don't need an image that you created in order to reach Destiny. You are created in the image of God, and that's the only image that matters.

Many people choose to invest their time in looking like they've made it, rather than investing time in the things that will help them achieve genuine success. They invest in depreciating assets so that they can "keep up with the Joneses," only to find their house repossessed. Is it more important to have the latest luxury car or to send your children to college?

Prioritize your spending so you can be free to travel the road of Destiny. You can't be free to pursue Destiny if you're a slave to debt and spending. Choosing to live your dream may mean quitting your job to pursue your calling. But if you're up to your ears in debt, you can't walk away from that job. If you owe everybody in town, you'll never save enough money to buy the dream home you want. Your dream may be to send your children to a private school to broaden their opportunities, but you probably can't afford it if you're spending money on the latest style of athletic shoes or expensive kids' birthday parties that your children may not even remember.

Prioritize how your money is spent and be a good steward of the financial blessings you have already received, no matter how meager. Show God you can be trusted with the small amount given you, and the Almighty Provider will give you more. If you're wasteful with small sums of money, you'll be wasteful with large sums, too.

Prioritize What's Important for *You* to Fulfill *Your* Dream

It's miserable living someone else's life, and it is downright suffocating to live beneath your potential. There is no reward in achieving someone else's plans for your life, yet people will constantly try to suck you into their agenda. Other people always have an opinion about what you should do with your life. Your mother may think you should teach school because that's a vocation that represents a steady paycheck. Your father may nag you about going to medical school because you earned good grades in science. Your best friend thinks you should open a day care because you're good with children. Your grandmother tells you to start a newspaper because you are a good writer. All of those vocations are great and the service they give to humanity is quite valuable. The problem is that if the vocation is not reflective of your destiny, it's no good.

Believe it or not, some have never been allowed to prioritize their own lives. There's a son who longs to sculpt, but because his parents are both PhDs, they use parental pressure to steer him to a vocation that is more palatable to them. There's a daughter who loves cars and dreams of being a master mechanic, but her boyfriend has discouraged her because he doesn't think it's suitable work for a woman. Set your priorities for Destiny and forget about what other people want for you, no matter how well-meaning their intentions.

Only you can have the vision for your life, so only you can determine what's most important to getting there. Other people may not understand or respect the sacrifices you choose to make on your way to Destiny, but don't ever let that stop you. Your choices won't make sense to anyone else because they can't see what you can see. They don't know where you're going. Sometimes your choices won't even make sense to the people you love most, but those who truly love you will respect your priorities, even if they don't understand them.

Your priorities confirm where you're headed because everything you do will be in support of your destination. A person who has priorities will drive an older or a cheaper car, will forgo designer label clothing, and will pass up the latest model of an electronic device if she has a dream that requires keeping tight control on her finances. When a young man's priorities are in place, he will skip going to shoot some hoops with his buddies in order to spend an extra hour on a school project. A woman will pass on that vacation with the girls because her fiancé wants her to go to his family reunion. A man will stay on the job that will give him the training he needs for a sustainable future rather than take a higher-paying dead-end job. A couple will opt for a less expensive wedding in order to have more money for a substantial down payment on their new house.

People who are living life on purpose have priorities and tend to get more out of life. They are happier, even in difficult times, because they have a reason to exist. They know why they've made certain choices, so they don't feel like victims for living a less-than-impressive lifestyle. They live in pursuit of Destiny rather than in pursuit of other people's approval.

Cultivate a Great Mind and Leave Behind Small Thinking

If you don't prioritize your life and the things that are important to you, you'll get off focus and start investing your energy in trivial matters like who lied to you, who's gossiping about you, or who's gossiping about someone else. America's former first lady Eleanor Roosevelt observed that "Great minds discuss ideas; average minds discuss events; small minds discuss people." You are the one who determines your thoughts. You are the one who determines the issues that are worthy of your time. You have the power to push aside pettiness in pursuit of greatness.

Your destiny is greatness. Pettiness and greatness cannot occupy the same space. Don't block Destiny opportunities from manifesting in your life because you're prioritizing minor issues. If your aunt and your cousin are fighting again, let them work out their own problems because Destiny is calling you! If your neighbor refuses to abide by the rules of your homeowners association, let it go. Destiny is calling you. If your sourpuss employee does a good job, let it go. As long as she's not dealing with the public, the fact that she doesn't have a bubbly personality is a minor issue. If someone you were depending on backs out of a business deal, don't spend a lot of time figuring out why. That's minor. You need to be looking for a new partner. That's major.

Greatness runs deep, but pettiness runs shallow and wide. Petty thinking is a fast-moving carcinogen that will spread itself over the greatness in you and eat away at your potential for growth. Stop allowing minor thoughts to occupy your mind; they're not paying rent to reside there!

Reserve your strength for the difficult matters of arriving at

Destiny. There's some stuff you just leave alone. You don't fix every problem that comes across your radar. You don't try to straighten out every dispute that comes before you. Don't chase down every rumor. If people are gossiping about you, let them talk, because the people who are talking negatively about you don't matter.

It is dangerous to let minor matters become priorities because when major things happen, you won't have the strength and fortitude needed to deal with what's important. Save your strength and don't toss and turn at night over minor issues. Don't dredge up negative experiences and expend mental energy ruminating over them. Don't worry about why that person didn't speak to you, why they lied to you, why they didn't invite you to their event. Reserve your energy for your highest and best use!

If you are ever to connect with Destiny, you must develop the art of handling minor issues appropriately. Many things happen at the Potter's House that I never even know about. My staff knows not to tell me because they know I'll get involved in it and try to figure out a solution. I'm glad I have a capable staff that can handle the day-to-day issues that crop up. They know that my time is limited and I can't afford to get distracted by minor problems. But that means something else, too. We hire smart people at the Potter's House. I can't hire limited thinkers. I can't hire mediocre people whom I'm smarter than so they can make me feel superior. No, I have to hire people who are smarter than me at what they do so I can walk away knowing those people can be trusted to do the job. I've known managers, CEOs, and company owners who get intimidated by people who are smarter than they are. They hire persons of mediocre or very average capability so they will always feel like they're on top. Hiring smart people makes me feel like I'm on top because I can focus on the tasks that are uniquely mine to accomplish.

I don't have to worry about having enough toner for the copy machine or what time the bank deposit got there. I have prioritized and determined that my time is best spent on my destiny, not on keeping track of what everyone else is doing.

Destiny's Diminutive Beginnings

When your priorities are set toward Destiny, you are aware of where you are and where you are trying to go. And because you are aware, you are prepared to seize opportunities as they arise. You won't be so blinded by the big picture that you can't see the smaller scenarios along the way. Pay attention to the small things because sometimes the greatest opportunity can come through seemingly insignificant events. Sometimes the daily bus ride to work introduces you to your spouse. Sometimes a volunteer position in an organization connects you to the CEO of the company you've been longing to work for. The Bible encourages us not to despise small beginnings; they often lead to greatness.

Greatness has to marinate. The age of television and movies can give the impression that fame is captured and notoriety is gained in an hour of programming or a few weeks of a reality show. And yes, many people have become well-known fairly quickly because of reality television shows, but there's still no such thing as an overnight success. Every person who attains significance in his or her field of endeavor had to pay some dues to get there—working low-paying jobs, working for free as an intern or volunteer, or giving faithful service on a job even while the boss takes the credit.

God has ordered our existence to operate like a farmer planting seed in a field. If you pray and ask God for an oak tree, the

Almighty might send you an acorn, because big things can come from small beginnings. God's answer may not look like your request. So when you get an acorn but were expecting a tree, don't throw the acorn away. Your tree is in the seed. God works through the agricultural principle of planting a seed and reaping a harvest. Your something small can become something mighty if you are a good steward of the seed.

Flexibility Keeps You from Breaking

Some people have no problem prioritizing and setting their affairs in order. If anything, they're too good at putting things in order. They must live in such a way that everything is in its place and nothing is out of place. We all experience moments when everything is perfectly ordered, but life is just not like that all the time. Things change. Life changes. You change. Your life cannot remain static. You are a living, breathing organism. And in order to get where God wants you to be, you can't stay where you are.

Order is essential, but life is full of changes. Sometimes life does not always fit a certain order. People come and go in your life. One minute you have a job and the next minute you've been laid off. One day everybody is doing fine and the next day someone in the family is diagnosed with a terminal illness.

Life is full of change. A man can be on a great career path—great salary, regular raises, promotions, and recognitions. He can be a rising star until something happens. The company folds or downsizes. A new CEO comes in and there's a personality clash. It's change, and you have to adapt.

People respond differently to challenging times. It's always a jolt when life sends us a tumble-and-fall moment. But what do you do when you get knocked down? A person whose priorities are set doesn't let one knockdown keep her from Destiny. Instead, she dusts herself off and gets back on the journey, ever observant for subtle changes and signs that indicate Destiny may be found in a totally different direction.

Maya Angelou often talked about her grandmother, like I often talk about mine. She told how she admired her grandmother for carving a new path for her life when the road she was on got cut short. Annie Henderson's marriage failed in a time when people simply didn't divorce. She had two young children, one physically disabled, and she needed to earn a living.

Annie wasn't educated but could read well enough and had a decent ability with numbers. Getting a job at one of the local mills was out of the question. She adapted herself to the prejudices with which a Negro woman in her day had to contend, and she found a way for herself and her family.

She began selling fresh hot meat pies to the men working at the mills. She set up outside the mill and began frying as soon as the noon bell rang. Over the years she built a loyal following and erected a stall nearby to sell her pies. In the years to come, her little stall evolved into a general store, where she traded with black and white customers alike. Maya recalled that from her grandmother she learned that when life sends us down an ominous road, we must look around and, without embarrassment, pick a new one.

It's difficult to continue moving in faith toward Destiny when life doesn't go the way you'd planned. One of the hardest things for people to do is to trust and believe God when in transition. You lose a loved one. The marriage you thought would last forever dies. It's devastating when you lose your job or lose a loved one or experience betrayal by someone you considered a good friend.

After the initial shock of loss, a typical human response after a disruptive experience is to restore a sense of order. We quickly try to restore or replace what was lost. An unemployed person takes the first job offered, whether or not it's a career fit. A widowed person quickly remarries.

Yet there are times when emptiness is needed so that God can be allowed to fill the void. God cannot fill a vessel that is already full. God uses empty vessels. Trust God to fill the void created when things don't go as you planned. Human beings can find all kinds of ways to fill the void of loss, and many of them are not good. Substance abuse, compulsive shopping, compulsive spending, excessive eating, sexual promiscuity, and reckless choices are just a few of the unhealthy ways we can attempt to fill a void.

God can use disorder to create a new order in your life. Sometimes disruptions actually serve to order our chaotic circumstances and take us to a new place. Like the mother eagle that stirs her nest to bring discomfort to her brood, God sometimes stirs up our lives. The shifts and setbacks you experience are not necessarily the work of your opposers. Sometimes a setback is a divine setup. Chaos on the outside actually may be God clearing out conditions, situations, or people that are in the way of your path to Destiny. But it's hard to ride the wave when it seems like a life storm will overtake you. It's hard to trust that God is in control of your circumstances even during tumultuous times.

It's easy to see what God was doing in your life once you get to the place God intended. The difficulty lies in seeing by faith what God is doing when you're on your way there. When you arrive at the place where God intended for you to be, you can say, "Okay, I see what was going on now." Nobody likes hard times, but it's the unpleasant experiences that are often the catalysts to build the character required for our destiny.

Let go of your desire to control what you cannot know, change, or control. Let go of the past. Let go of your fear. Let go of your pain. The systems that worked for you in the past will not work for you in the place where God is leading you. When you learn not to define yourself by where you were, you learn not to call the transitions in your life change. Instead, they're called normal, and you are a full participant in the movements of your life. Your normal should be constantly calibrating yourself and letting go of who you were to embrace who you are becoming.

Determine that you will remain open to where you are being led and are willing to take responsibility for the transitions that lead you to Destiny.

CHAPTER 5

Focus—Decide What Deserves You

Step toward What's Worth Your Time and Energy

You are not what you do. Arriving at Destiny involves separating yourself from your gift. Many times people confuse who you are with what you do. Differentiating between who you are and what you do is critical for your well-being. As I've traveled in inner circles with highly visible people and gotten to know them personally, I have often found that an individual is totally different from what is broadcast on TV or in public forums. Your favorite comedian may not be nearly as jovial offstage as when the cameras are rolling. They are giving their gift and talent to the audience, but that is not an indication of who they are in their daily lives or how they may be feeling. In that same way, you can use your gift, but that doesn't mean you *are* the gift.

Many are drawn to what you do, what you know, or some

gift you have and will be totally oblivious to the person you are. You don't have to be famous or on television to understand the distinction.

Your Gifts Make Room for You

If you're a very gifted person, people will seek you out. They will call upon you constantly to share your gifts for one purpose or another. There's a wonderful promise in the Bible, in Proverbs 18:16, that says your gifts will make room for you and propel you to higher places. It is a beautiful unfolding as your gifts open doors for you to run a corporation, play basketball, write, paint, remodel, practice medicine, teach, cook, or nurture—whatever you are gifted to do. When you are really good at your gift and work to hone your skills, people will constantly request your services. Being sought after can make you feel loved and admired. It can make you feel worthy. But don't confuse the gift with you.

People see me preach on television every week and feel they know me. One lady ran up to me one day while I was out shopping and said, "I know who you are!"

"You do?" I asked.

She smiled widely and replied, "You're the guy on *Oprah*!"

To someone else I am the pastor of a megachurch. To others I am a movie producer, a philanthropist, a businessman. I learned to be careful not to allow how others define me to become how I see myself. My self and my service are not the same thing. They know Bishop T.D. Jakes. They don't know Thomas Dexter Jakes, the man.

I don't get it twisted and neither should you. Just because people love your gift doesn't mean they love you. Most of them will never really know you. Most of them don't care about you. They just want your gift. And it's okay to share your gift. It's a good thing to serve your gift to people or in places that may benefit from it.

There may be occasions when both your service and your self agree and you are fully invested in that arena. For example, I have invested my self in the Potter's House, not only my gift. That is the place to which God called me, and I'm all in. I have learned that I am most powerful and effective when I am fully invested.

On the journey to Destiny, be aware that you may share your gift and not share you. Make that distinction so people who constantly want something from you will not drain you. People can drain you by continuously asking you to give and give and give, perhaps without the slightest concern for the personal toll it takes on you. Be prepared to set boundaries of how far, how much, and how long you are going to pour into others. You may think, as I did: "Oh, I have to do it. They love me." But actually, they love your gift and how that gift serves their purposes. The gift doesn't shine if the giver is extinguished!

Decide to step into your destiny by determining not only where you will share your gifts, but also where you are going to be all in—investing your self and your service. If you spend your self and your service where your service alone would be enough, you are not as energized to perform on the level you need to move closer into Destiny. You will have wasted the grace you have been given on assignments that aren't in alignment with where you are destined to go! I learned that in order to move the Richter scale of your success toward Destiny you have to be fully invested, and you can't be fully invested in everything and everyone you meet. There's simply not enough of you to go around!

Destiny Always Pays Its Bills

There are seasons in life when, in order to reach Destiny, you may have to donate both your service and your self. When those seasons arise, be sure that it is a step on the road to Destiny, because ultimately Destiny will always pay its bills. It will always pay you back! I remember how my mother helped me as a young man buy books and ministry materials. I was taking classes and courses, preaching, teaching, and being taught. One of our relatives chastened my mother for helping me. She said, "Don't spend all your money backing that boy!" I'm sure my aunt meant well and was only trying to protect my mother. What she didn't understand is that Destiny always pays its bills.

Understand the value of your efforts and be fully prepared to sow before you harvest, to give before you receive. Give the seed of your time, your energy, and even your self. But do not try to grow a garden on concrete! Destiny always pays you back, but every deal that's offered to you, every request from you, and every need that comes across your desk may not be a seed planted in the garden of Destiny. Instead, many are thrust upon the cold concrete of endless demands from people who only take!

Decide how and where to invest in you. There are times when you should do something for nothing. Yes, by all means be generous; but be smart. Balance the call to give with the understanding that the gifts God has given you are worth something. Pay your dues on the way to Destiny, but somewhere along the way Destiny begins to pay you back dividends. That's why you have to determine who and what deserves you. With every opportunity, gauge how you can maximize your exposure. An invitation to sing at a benefit concert should be the gig that puts you before a record label executive or an artist recruitment scout. Writing free for a local paper should help you accumulate some bylines to build a portfolio and get paying assignments. Don't simply share your gifts because you believe people will love you for it. Your gifts are worthy of recognition, worthy of remuneration, worthy of advancement. Remember, the consumer never sets the price on the product!

I'm not talking about giving up personal fulfillment and purpose. I'm talking about people who pull on you over and over again, suck up your time and energy, and do not give you room to grow.

Just because you share yourself in the same place continuously doesn't mean it's a dead end. If preparing income tax forms for a beloved nonprofit organization is a fulfillment of Destiny, by all means do that until you drop. If volunteering your services to the children's hospital is how you choose to give back, that's great, too! Be generous until your generosity comes at the expense of your destiny! Remember, Destiny always pays its bills—and gives you returns.

Destiny Is Worth Fighting For

The things that are most important in life often do not come without challenge or struggle. Nobody likes to lose, but that doesn't mean every conflict or struggle you encounter in life is worth a fight. When we see something slipping away from our grasp, our instinct is to go into fight mode to protect and preserve what belongs to us. A threat to our career means a fight. A threat to our home means a fight. A threat to our marriage or our health means it's time to fight. The willingness and readiness to fight off a threat is a healthy trait. But some situations simply are not worth a fight.

Sometimes a pink slip on the job is the best thing that could happen to boost your career advancement in another setting. Rejection from a lover may pull the plug on a relationship that's been on life support for too many years. The repossession of the car you couldn't afford may be your ticket to economic freedom and redemption.

At first, these kinds of situations can stir you into fight mode. But fighting for something that is inconsequential in the grand scheme of your destiny can hold you back from attaining what you really desire. On a deeper, spiritual level, survival may actually mean letting go of what's been holding you back. Very often, knowing whether it's time to fight or let go is a matter of putting your ego in check and out of the way.

Let's say you find out a guy named Rick is pursuing your girlfriend, the woman you've given four hundred different excuses as to why you two are not ready to marry. But now that another man is trying to move in on your relationship, you're ready to fight. Maybe Rick is the best thing for you and for your girlfriend. Maybe Rick wants to marry her and give her the kind of relationship she desires. Maybe it's time for you to get your ego out of the way and move on to your destiny.

Have you ever been embroiled in a fight and later realized that it was all about ego? How dare they terminate me? Who is he to break up with me? They can't talk to me like that and get away with it! Ego fights are often ugly, vicious, and unreasonable. But when you fight for a true cause, like your destiny, you make reasonable and sound decisions because it's not really about you. It's about your call to serve humanity. Conversely, when your fight is about ego, you can make all kinds of stupid, irrational decisions because the ego tells you that the only thing that's important is you.

Sometimes we fight the wrong battles because of displaced anger. You can't fight with your boss at work so you come home and fight with your spouse or your children. You can't fight with your spouse so you take it out on your church members and fight about meaningless, trivial matters. You can't fight the health condition or the financial downturn so you fight with the salesperson who won't argue back.

Some fights you get sucked into are really other people's struggles. People who are afraid of fighting for themselves can be masters at manipulating others into fighting for them. Before you get ready to do battle, make sure you're fighting your own battles for your own meaningful and worthwhile purpose.

Time is a precious commodity and it must be used carefully and judiciously. Your time is worth everything. Time is your greatest weapon, so choose the situations and circumstances that are worth fighting for. Don't waste your time fighting meaningless battles. Meaningless combat won't help your future. Invest your time where it matters.

On the way to Destiny, know that there will be battles to fight. Know that what you're fighting for is worth it. Your children, your marriage, your career are always worth fighting for, but even then, you may come to a point when you have to give up an active fight and just let God fight the battle for you.

Focus Will Sustain Your Passion

The walk toward Destiny is a trek of endurance. Every day is not exciting, even when you are doing what you love. Working toward your destiny is a daily endeavor, but every moment will not be filled with thrills, or even challenge. Some days are just clocking hours of work. But when you know why you're working, why you're sacrificing, or why you're delaying gratification, you can sustain your passion for where you are going, especially when your goal seems lodged in a stratosphere you will never reach.

Destiny is a long-distance race where endurance is the key to winning. On the journey we get weak in body and in mind sometimes. We get sick and tired. We get sick and tired of being sick and tired. We grow weary from a tiredness that often is not physical; sometimes we get emotionally, mentally, or spiritually weary. Circumstances we thought would have been resolved years before may continue to haunt us.

Sometimes we feel like we don't have anything else to give, even to Destiny. We've given all that we have and we ask ourselves, "What more do our children want? What more does my spouse want from me? What more does my employer expect of me?" Meanwhile life goes on, leaving us feeling both overwhelmed and underwhelmed: overwhelmed by mounting pressures because life and livelihood have to be maintained; underwhelmed because nothing seems to be changing for the better. Destiny is a distant place that seems unreachable.

It takes determination to continue operating in the day-to-day while keeping a healthy focus on Destiny. Help yourself and develop connections with people who are already at or near the place you want to be. Learn from them because being around them can help you stay focused on why you're making sacrifices and enduring struggles.

People who love what they do and are successful at it tend to enjoy establishing relationships with serious mentees. They love to share stories of their setbacks and successes, their trials and triumphs. They want to encourage a protégé to keep getting better at the gift. Mentors can often advise you regarding actions that may not be a productive payoff. They may be able to help you recognize a dead-end employment situation or tell when it's time to let a business relationship go. Sometimes the best hello to a new opportunity is the good-bye you gave to a dead situation.

"You'll Win If You Don't Quit!"

I learned that quitters don't win when I faced formidable circumstances and complex dilemmas. More than a few times, I felt my faith give way and my heart become faint. I remember trying to get a loan for a piece of property for our church in West Virginia. It seemed that at every turn I ran into an obstacle. I had applied at different banks. Some said no; others required 40 percent down (which was still a no because I didn't have it). I carried the cross of their rejection silently. I didn't want the church to know that our dream was my nightmare.

I reasoned the church could stay where it was, even though the space was too small. I sometimes wondered if it would be better to let go of the pain of wanting and settle for the calm mediocrity of the status quo. But after every rejection my passion would revitalize and I would try again. Whether I was secretly masochistic or had faith, I wasn't sure. I was not certain I had the right approach or the right business acumen, but unbeknownst to me, I was attaining my business acumen through the rejection process! The pain of the process ultimately empowered me to acquire the property. Yes, I did get the loan and we purchased the building. But the greater gift was the experience. I learned to persevere, even in the tempestuous, arduous, agonizing *becoming* stage.

The West African Ashanti people say, "If you understand the beginning well, the end will not trouble you." When you are sure that you are aimed toward Destiny, you will not worry about the end. Instead, dig in your heels and hold on for the ride, with all of its highs and lows. Admittedly, tough times can make you want to run for the nearest exit. Keep in mind that those who figure out how to slide their way past difficulties do not meet their God-appointed destiny. Destiny belongs to those who demand it by their faithful and dogged determination to hang in there until they achieve what they desire.

Tyler Perry, famed playwright, director, actor, and producer, made his own way to Hollywood filmmaking, a circuitous route that would have caused many to give up. During his early years of positioning himself toward Destiny, the road was neither smooth nor accommodating to this young black man from New Orleans's Seventh Ward. In the toughest times, Tyler fought the fights that were worth pursuing and let go of the fights that were counterproductive to Destiny.

Starting at age twenty-two, Tyler wrote, directed, and produced many stage plays that were financed with his personal savings. For more performances than he could count, only a handful of people showed up. This went on for years. He continued to save and invest his own money to produce the plays, but nothing seemed to take off. Even when the cast performed to a nearly empty house, Tyler never let go of his dream. He battled all obstacles to produce another play, even when no one had come to the previous one.

Later, after some success with his plays, he stayed in the fight when Hollywood executives told him, ridiculously, they couldn't back his movie because "Black people don't go to the movies." He held on and refused to let go of his dream to write, direct, and produce plays and movies.

As Tyler fought for his place among filmmakers, he chose to let go of the fights that were counterproductive to Destiny. He could have spent his life fighting a father who ridiculed him. He could have engaged in a lifelong emotional battle against the people who sexually abused him. Instead, he invested his Warrior Spirit in fights that were worth the effort to get his plays and films to audiences. Tyler kept on fighting to live his dream, even when he was homeless and sleeping in his automobile. Because he never gave up, the winds of fate changed in his favor and he has since sold millions of theater and movie tickets to fans of his beloved Madea persona and the characters in his many other film and theatrical productions.

That's the kind of fight that's worth your energy. The fighting spirit in you that says, "I will..." is the tenacity you need to dig in deeper when friends and loved ones are looking at you and snickering because it seems like you've just been following a pipe dream for years. You've got another plan to make it big. You've started on another diet. You've started dating someone new. Meanwhile, the people around you are saying, "Uh-oh. Here we go again."

Ignore them and keep fighting because you are headed to a place they cannot see; stop expecting them to understand why you're willing to hold on and not let go. As they laugh or cluck their tongues, strengthen yourself to dig your heels in deeper. Don't tell them your dream. Sarcasm and doubt from other people can weaken your staying power. If you listen to enough of their vitriol, you will start to believe that you really are stupid for hanging on when there seems to be no reason.

Any person who has achieved success arrived at a pivotal point when he or she had to decide to keep going despite failures, despite negative future forecasts, despite haters who couldn't understand what it means to be focused on Destiny. There's a critical point that every successful person reaches when they say, "I'm going to stay right here and make this work or die trying."

Storms, Struggles, Battles, and Destiny

Storms and struggles can have a definite positive result on us because as discombobulating as they are, life's challenges can make us stronger to fulfill our destiny. But you can't live in fight mode; living that way is unhealthy and counterproductive. There's a reason soldiers are given leave time for rest and relaxation.

Fighting keeps you strong, but all of life is not about storms and battles. People who live in fight mode can die early from strokes or heart attacks because of constant stress on the body. There are times when you need to take off your armor and let your spirit be at peace. Develop habits that can release you from fight mode and give your mind and body a much-needed break. Yoga, meditation, or a brisk walk are just a few ways you can take care of yourself and ensure that you will live to fight another day.

In a professional boxing match, the two opponents fight for three-minute rounds. They then retreat to their respective corners for sixty seconds of respite, encouragement, and strategizing. The fighter must take a quick break so he can get back up and fight again. In the corner, the fighter's team is tending to his wounds, nurturing him, telling him where he's vulnerable, and affirming his strong points.

Can you imagine how truly brutal a professional boxing match would be if the two opponents fought for a full thirty-six minutes with no break in the competition? Prior to the mid-eighteenth century, there were no rules for boxers, and many died in the ring. The first rules for boxing, known as Broughton's rules, were established by champion Jack Broughton to protect fighters. He realized that rules were needed so that the boxers could live to fight another day.

Establish personal rules for taking care of yourself. There will be more storms to endure on the way to Destiny. There will be more battles to fight. After you have seen your way through a storm, take some time for yourself and your family. Take time to celebrate that the storm has passed without worrying about when the next one will come. That will come soon enough.

Times of calm are times to appreciate the victory or soothe the wounds of defeat. Getting out of fight mode gives you time to plan and strategize taking your steps to the next level. It's the time to thank your spouse or your family for being your support system in the storm. It's the time to be in touch with yourself and remind yourself that you are a human being and not a human doing.

CHAPTER 6

For Destiny's Sake, Do You!

Take Steps toward Authentic Self-Identity

Destiny is the ultimate expression of doing you, fully being yourself, making your own choices. No one else can do what you do. Other people may have your talent, but they don't have your twist.

Doing you yields the ultimate in life satisfaction because it means engaging every fiber of your being into your destiny. If you're bored with life, it's probably because you're not doing you. How could you possibly be bored if you are doing what the Creator put you on this earth to accomplish? If you're sarcastic and negative about life, you're not doing you. There's no way to have a negative view of life if you have engaged your best self to complete the task God designed for you. God created sun, moon, stars, and seasons. Surely there is something in this vast universe that would interest you if you were on your authentic path to Destiny.

It should be exciting to think about doing you. How could you not be excited about the fact that God created you? If you are not doing you, you're like a racehorse that has never been put on the track. You're a 350-horsepower engine that's stored in a garage collecting dust. Allow Destiny to reveal what you are truly made of by discovering what it means to do you!

You'd Like to Get to Know You

"Know thyself" is an aphorism that originated among the ancient Greeks. Inscribed on the Temple of Apollo at Delphi, the maxim figures prominently in Greek literature, especially the writings of the philosopher Plato and his teacher Socrates. It is from Plato's writings that we learn Socrates's quote: "The unexamined life is not worth living." The pursuit of our life's destiny is how we discover who we really are.

It is in the pursuit of Destiny that you discover what a fascinating person you are. You discover that you are an amazing and unique creation of God. As you get to know yourself, you find out some things you want to change, but you will also discover some things you like. Self-discovery can be a deeply rewarding life process, as you learn to embrace truths that others told you about yourself and release the lies that beat down your self-esteem.

You may learn that Aunt Kaye was right when she said you had a knack for getting at the real issue in a conflict. Maybe Destiny is calling you to be a mediator, a negotiator, an attorney, or a judge. You may also discover that some hurtful words said about you were untrue—the parent who called you dumb or the teacher who said you didn't have the aptitude to go to college.

Get to know you. Knowing you may mean discovering that while everyone thought you were moody and cranky, you're really an introvert who just needs a little time away from people to regenerate your internal energy. Or maybe you're an extrovert who was accused of having ants in your pants because you couldn't seem to keep still. You craved the connection with other human beings. Getting to know who you really are means you equip yourself to take care of you in the ways that help you become your best self.

When you get to know you, your likes and dislikes, your passions and your plans, your motivators and your downers become evident. Knowing you means you simultaneously learn what it takes to inspire you to Destiny. It's a disclosure that happens quickly for some and more slowly for others. Some people move toward Destiny like shooting stars while others are late bloomers, but it is a lifelong unfolding.

Some seem to be born knowing who they are and what they are destined to contribute, while others stumble from one life post to another, trying to figure out what they want to be when they grow up. Some people overcome incredible odds and pass through hell and high water to meet up with Destiny. Others are given every economic, educational, and social advantage yet slip into an abyss of unproductivity. It all comes down to one thing: know thyself.

People who grew up in poverty may have to learn who they are apart from an environment filled with street-corner drug deals, substandard housing, high incarceration rates, high teen pregnancy rates, and low expectations. If you grew up this way, your environment may tell you that you are destined to sell drugs, but actually, you love to write science fiction. Get in touch with the real you so that you can see your higher self and realize your ability to distance from the negative realities of a dysfunctional upbringing. If you grew up poor, take time to get to know your higher self, the one who has Destiny that does not include incarceration, drugs, and unplanned pregnancy. Distinguish your true self from the environment where you grew up.

You have to know yourself to live the authentic life that Destiny offers you. Otherwise, you can have outward success and not fully experience the fruit of your accomplishments. You can be a self-made millionaire who runs a company and wears thousand-dollar suits but still see yourself as that little girl who was made fun of at school for wearing thrift-store clothes. You may still be living like the little boy whose parent never had money to give him for extracurricular activities at school. You were never to be defined by those circumstances. That was where you lived, not who you are. You can graduate at the top of your class at Harvard yet still doubt whether you are successful because your father never affirmed or encouraged your accomplishments.

No matter what kind of upbringing or past experiences you had, you can benefit from distinguishing your past from your authentic self. You can learn from it and distance yourself from it in a healthy way. You may have been raised by parents who held conservative religious or political values that you do not share. Acknowledge the positive values they gave you, and then embrace the values that represent you, that support you, and that help steer you toward Destiny. You can't deny where you came from, but you can learn from it, grow from it, and build upon it to take you higher.

How we were raised, where we went to school, and our social and economic experiences have a tremendous impact on us. Along the road to Destiny, you have to give yourself reality checks so the you that you know catches up to the you that you have become.

J.K. Rowling, author of the phenomenally successful Harry Potter series, was once clinically depressed and living on welfare in Scotland. She shared in an interview with Oprah Winfrey that she was still striving to know herself. It had been many years since she fought to scrape together sustenance for her and her child, but the struggling single mother she knew so well still held the power to overtake the billionaire author she has become. She recalled trying to finish the last Potter book in the series of seven. Children, family pets, and service workers had taken over the household and were breaking her concentration. At that point she connected with her new truth that she could afford to travel anywhere she wanted to complete the book. In her early years, she did her writing in local cafés, mostly because they were warmer than her cold apartment and sitting there didn't cost her any money. The single mother had to catch up to the billionaire to realize that she could afford to pay for a hotel for as long as she needed one. Her mind told her she still needed to watch every penny.

"Know thyself" doesn't apply only in moving from poverty to wealth. A person who grows up wealthy may be inflexible in situations where humility is their requisite for elevation to Destiny. The person who has always had financial abundance to address a problem may not be aware that there are some places money cannot take you and some situations that money cannot buy you into or out of. Wealth can lure you into a sense of entitlement that may hinder the arrival of Destiny, which cannot be bought. Destiny can take you to places where money is insufficient to give you entrance.

Put That Down! It's Not Yours, Anyway

When you take the time to get to know yourself, you don't run the risk of living someone else's dream. Self-knowledge will allow you to appreciate and admire someone else's dream and cheer them on to Destiny as it unfolds for them. Knowing thyself means you can celebrate with your coworker who just got a promotion at the company where you're simply passing through. The promotion is their dream, not yours. But if you don't know yourself, you might become jealous, confused, or angry, asking, "Why did Amanda get the promotion? I've got more education than her, and a broader skill set, too." What difference does it make? That's not your dream; it's your coworker's. If you're working for a while at a retail chain, be happy that Greg got promoted to management. You may be smarter, more educated, and have more experience, too. But if retail management is not your destiny, giving you a promotion there would only make you and everyone around you miserable.

What works for someone else simply won't work for you. Do the work required for your own life and stay away from other people's dreams. Don't be jealous or insecure about other people's accomplishments. God has an abundant storehouse of blessings for you as the God-destined life for you unfolds. Knowing thyself means you can be happy for your BFF when she gets married, even while you wait for your Mr. Right. Knowing you means you can be genuinely happy for the person who earns another degree, moves into their dream house, or buys that head-turner of a sports car.

Destiny is smart and she doesn't make mistakes. You can try all you want to live someone else's destiny, but it just won't fit. You'll never flow in what you do by living someone else's dream, and it will never feed your soul. It doesn't matter how good it looks if you get the dream job and all the perks that go along with it, if you get the eye-candy woman on your arm, or the Nobel Prize, or the scholarship to Harvard, or the home in a gated community—if something isn't a part of your destiny, it cannot bring you fulfillment.

Have you ever known someone who seemed to have everything, yet they never look happy? I mean *everything.* A man can wear expensive tailored suits, live in the city's most desirable neighborhood, and have a beautiful family of Rhodes Scholars who've never caused their parents a day's trouble. Those are all wonderful accomplishments for which anyone should be grateful, but if that man is not living Destiny, there's a big hole someplace. The big hole is why your next-door neighbor can be driving a Mercedes to a job she despises and start hating on you as you happily drive an old pickup truck to make deliveries for your own business.

When you live your own dream, you don't have time to be a hater. You can't even think like a hater, because all of that negative energy will just bring you down. You need all of your energy for Destiny. Don't waste it on someone else. When you are fulfilled in pursuit of Destiny, you're good and you want everyone else to be good with themselves, too.

If you know thyself, you'll be better equipped to identify and extract your authentic needs from what you've been told you need. A consumer who knows thyself will be able to distinguish an authentic need from a conditioned need and bypass the latest new product release if the one she has is adequate for her needs. When you are in touch with your own pursuit of Destiny, you seek the things you need to accomplish what you desire. That's not to the exclusion of wants; please don't misunderstand. I'm not asking you to consider a life of only basic needs. I do not want to see you living in agony surrounded by accoutrements that weigh you down rather than build you up.

Invest in Doing You!

Are you trying to harvest an opulent life from a dollar-store investment in yourself? Destiny cannot be tricked by cheap imitations. When I had written my first book, I carried the manuscript from publisher to publisher and no one seemed remotely interested.

Just when I was about to trash the idea of being an author, an unusual opportunity was presented to me. The publisher said, "We will publish the book." But I would have to pay for the publishing! I would have to self-publish! It would cost me $15,000! My wife and I discussed it. We had the money. But it was *all* the money we had been saving for a house. After much prayer, we took the plunge and invested the money into the book. That book was *Woman, Thou Art Loosed*! It remains my highest-selling book! It has sold millions of copies and continues to bring life and hope to people today. But my literary life would never have seen the light of day if I hadn't been willing to invest in my own dream. Incidentally, though we had to put the house on hold for a while, we soon were blessed to purchase a much better one than what we'd expected to buy initially!

While it is true that Destiny is a compulsive flirt, don't ever allow her flirtations to make you think she is promiscuous. Those who have been with her will tell you she doesn't come cheap! You've got to show her that you are serious. Invest in doing you and don't have a cheap attack. Don't get the least amount of training, the least amount of education, or the least amount of skill. You can't give the least amount of effort and expect to find your way to Destiny. Go to the best school your finances and grades allow. Study hard and earn the best grades you're capable of getting. Take time to learn all you can about your job, even the things you think don't matter. Build a vast store of experiences that will develop a well-roundedness in you that will expand your possibilities for maximum living.

Investing in you requires sacrifice—your sacrifice. No one else can make certain sacrifices for you. (Parents may sacrifice to pay for your education, but no one else but you can give up the fun times to put time in for studying.) Everyone has a life and a calling to experience and no one else can make your dreams come true. It's not up to your parents, your spouse, your children, or your boss to make your life what you desire. They can all lend a hand and be your cheerleaders, but they can't make it happen for you.

Don't be a cheapskate! You and your dream are worth the price of admission into Destiny. If you don't invest in you, you'll soon find that no one else will, either. In fact, others may shy away from you if they feel you expect them to make your dream happen off their backs. Most people can tell when you're serious about what you want from life. They can tell if you're serious about being an actor, serious about being a software developer, serious about being a day-care owner. As people watch you make sacrifices to invest in yourself, they will want to invest in your dream, too. When you are busily engaged in personal investment, God sends people from out of nowhere to support you, encourage you, and invest in your dream. You may not even be aware that they're watching you, but they will show up and amaze you.

Investing in yourself requires determination—the kind that knows Destiny is worth never giving up. The determination you have to invest in you says that even if no one else believes in you, you do. Even if no one else can see what's inside you, you do. Be determined to invest in you despite delays, setbacks, sidetracks, and turnarounds.

Your personal investment requires commitment. Hang in there with Destiny, even when it isn't looking good for you.

Popular or unpopular, appreciated or not, encouraged or not, understood or not, hold on to Destiny and don't let go. Take a vow and declare your commitment to Destiny's unfolding in your life.

Personal investment requires exposure. Destiny will take you to new heights and you need to be ready. Put yourself in new and perhaps uncomfortable or intimidating environments. Invest in yourself by giving yourself new lessons in culture, history, art, theater, religion, geography, or whatever you need to expand your horizon.

You need tenacity to secure your investment in you. Pursing Destiny is not for wimps. You can't back down or cower away. You may be terrified when you're presented with some situations. But stick to investing in you despite your fears and you will overcome them.

You Play the Lead Role in Your Destiny

Value you. Imagine the world without you. Realize just how priceless you are. Think about the people whose lives you've touched, the things that would be different had you never lived. Your children would never have been born. The sibling you helped might never have gotten through college. Value the contribution of your life and the role that you still can play—a lead role. You play the lead role in your life. The mission that no one else can accomplish is yours. The task that no one else can complete is yours. The steps that no one else can navigate are yours to ascend. No one else can take your place.

I was just a boy when Dr. Martin Luther King Jr. was assassinated in 1968, but I recall that many were speculating about who would take his place. Names were circulated, and some tried to position themselves for the role, but he was irreplaceable.

Dr. King had a destiny that he fulfilled. No one could step into his shoes as the voice of the civil rights movement.

Like Dr. King or any other person we deem great, you are irreplaceable. No one can take your place to fulfill your destiny. This is your life. No rehearsals. No retakes. No delete button.

Understanding that you have been chosen to play the lead role in your life is a critical Destiny step.

CHAPTER 7

Maybe It's Time for a Reset

Change Your Step to Get in Step with Your Destiny

Do you have any idea who you have the capacity to become? If you were not bound by the confines of your mind, who might you become? What fields of endeavor might you pursue? If you didn't believe that you were limited, too unattractive, too ordinary, too broke, too tall, too fat, too short, too uneducated, too unpolished, or too whatever, what could possibly stop you from reaching out to Destiny? The human brain has about a million sensory receptors that manage the data that comes into our minds. Sometimes the receptors are skewed by negative experiences, socialization, or other Destiny blockers, and what we see in ourselves is not real.

What's going on in your head can seem more real to you than what actually exists. Singer-songwriter Ray Charles described his ability to hear and compose music in his head. Having gone blind as a boy, Charles's auditory abilities had become highly developed and sensitized. Brother Ray said that when he heard a tune in his head, he didn't need a piano to compose it because every part of the song was already completed in his head.

The human mind is a powerful processing machine. At best, that process is imagination and genius propelling us to new worlds. At worst, the distortions of the mind are mental illness. The mind can make you believe people are following you when no one is around. The mind can cause you to walk and carry yourself like you're Miss America when in reality your looks and your physique are rather ordinary.

It's usually a good thing when our minds can propel us beyond our present reality. Most people you and I admire probably found their purpose and calling by resisting the innate tendency to acquiesce to the circumstances around them. They may have been born poor but refused to be doomed by environmental conditions. Who would have imagined that a blind girl like Helen Keller would end up being a world-famous teacher? Or think of the many veterans who came home handicapped but refused to allow their physical limitations to enslave them. Instead, with tenacity and perseverance these brave men and women rose up to lead impressive lives!

Renowned journalist Bob Schieffer told me most of his greatest accomplishments occurred after he turned sixty-five! He admonished me not to allow age to deter my move forward. Destiny has no expiration date! A woman was lamenting to her friend that she'd never finished college. "I wish I'd stuck with it then, but it's too late." The friend asked, "What's stopping you?" The woman sighed. "It's going to take me six years because I can only go part-time. I'm forty-eight now. By the time I finished, I'd be fifty-four years old." The friend paused for a moment, then replied, "Well, how old will you be in six years if you don't go to college?" When you know you have not gone as far as Destiny wants to take you, age is little more than a number.

Many who have great accomplishments saw that person they became in themselves before they actually grew to be that person. They saw the actor before they ever stood in front of a camera, they saw the entertainer long before they stood on stage, they saw the preacher when there was no congregation, the business owner showed up before the articles of incorporation, the teacher showed up in their mind before they walked through the classroom doors, the vision of motherhood appeared before the baby was conceived.

The mind also can give you a negative, distorted image of self. People who battle with anorexia think they are overweight when they are literally skin and bones. I've met people who were incredibly talented but who could not see themselves as they really were. Their mind told them they were inadequate or limited.

Your mind is so strong and powerful, it can help you to overcome incredible obstacles and position you to become what you envision.

Take the Chain Off Your Brain

Have you considered whether your mind is open and free to explore the path that God has set for you? Or are you going through life like your brain is chained, locking in creativity and ideas? Free your mind and you will create a mental and spiritual environment for greatness. Examine yourself. Know what you believe. Know your ideas. Know what you stand for and know what has shaped your beliefs and ideas.

Consider your family upbringing and what you were taught to believe. You may need to take the chain off your brain to develop your own thought and belief systems. Your family may have prejudices or biases that you don't hold, but if you're walking around with the family chain on your brain, you may have restricted yourself to a narrow environment without room for people who think differently, who will position you toward Destiny. Take the chain off your brain and develop new associations. Build new friendships. Think new thoughts. Who you were raised to be will always have a significant impact on your life but does not have to determine your life and certainly doesn't have to restrict your life.

If you grew up with brothers and sisters, the dynamics of the household while you were growing up may shape each child differently. An alcoholic parent can raise identical twins. When they grow to adulthood, one becomes an alcoholic. Why? He might say, "Because I was raised by an alcoholic." The other twin is an absolute teetotaler. Why? He, too, might say, "Because I was raised by an alcoholic."

Whatever you have been through, whether heavenly or horrific, it will serve a meaningful purpose in your life if you allow it to. The pain you have been through, the losses, the humiliation, and the betrayal are all stepping-stones to a higher place in Destiny, if you are willing to take the chain off your brain.

My father's dream was for one of his sons to take over the family business. I understand why that was important to him. My dream would be for one of my children to take over what I had established also. But I learned from my own upbringing that forcing children to be a version of you for family continuity is not wise. My father had invested a great deal of himself into building a viable business that could support his progeny for generations. He wanted me to run a janitorial service. Many years later, my brother wanted me to join him in forming a windows and siding company, which I tried for a while and failed at miserably. If I had lived up to their expectations it would have been at the expense of my own purpose and destiny. There is no doubt in my mind that both my dad and my brother were really trying to help me. But good intentions don't indicate right directions. I was destined to be a communicator in various forms, like ministry, film, books, and television.

Do you have the courage to take the chain off your brain, even when the person who put it there is someone you love and who loves you? In spite of that love, they accidentally incarcerated your creativity. But prison is prison, whether intended or not.

Think about how you were reared—whether by a mother who worked as a waitress and could barely pay the rent in the trailer park where you lived, or whether you grew up like the Huxtable family of *The Cosby Show*, the popular television comedy of the 1980s and '90s. All of what you have experienced plays a role in Destiny, even the situations and people you must choose to leave behind in order to arrive there.

How to Reset

Think of your mind like a computer that occasionally has to be reset in order to perform optimally. When you reset an electronic device, it goes back to a default setting, but the default settings have to be changed for the device to get a new normal that yields optimal performance. Likewise, sometimes your perceptions of how the world operates have to change to give you a fresh perspective on your circumstances.

All of your experiences shape you into a unique person whom God can use to improve your life and someone else's, as you step into your destiny. And the experiences that influence us most are life's default settings. A child growing up in an abusive household can have a mental default set to "victim." If he's not intentional about changing, he will respond as the victim, even though he's now in adult situations. A child is deeply affected by growing up in poverty, and in adulthood when dealing in financial matters, is overly cautious with money or excessive in her spending. A man whose first wife left him for another man has a distrustful default setting in his future relationships. Without a reset, he will be unable to trust the woman in his life and may always be suspicious that she will cheat on him.

Sometimes entire families are caught in a dysfunctional default setting of relating to one another. Generation after generation falls into this cyclical trap and only a determined few make it out. No matter how many of your family members may be caught in a destructive cycle, you can decide to change and pursue your destiny. The only way to get off welfare is to change your default setting. The only way to get off drugs, to get out of a life of ignorance or violence, a life of mediocrity, or a life of depravity—none of these is your God-appointed destiny!—is to change your default setting.

Life's default settings are not necessarily negative. Our defaults can encourage positive behavior in us, too. When you regard yourself positively with high self-esteem, your default says that you are not the kind of person who cheats others, who abuses your spouse, who disrespects your elders, or who blows your rent money on a weekend in the Bahamas. Your default settings tell you, "I'm better than that," and steer you away from negative behavior. Don't reset good mental programming and mess yourself up.

Examine your thinking, your values, and your self-perception to get in touch with your current default and determine if it's time for an adjustment.

Your default will show you whether you are actively engaged

in doing you. If you don't consciously know what doing you means, you may be acting solely out of your default. Get to know you so that your actions are purposeful and deliberate toward Destiny. Here are five simple ways you can hit the reset button to reach your destiny!

1. **Social reset.** It may be time to reset some of your associations. That doesn't always mean dropping old friends as much as it may mean widening your repertoire of associates. Fresh contacts, fresh ideas, and fresh conversations all come from new associates. You will gain from resetting your relationship priorities.

2. **Spiritual reset.** It may be time to deepen your spiritual roots. Change your spiritual influence. Just because you are religious doesn't mean that you don't need to update your faith intake. Feeding your spirit is much like gassing up for a long trip. Spirituality is the gas that gets you to Destiny. If you aren't whole inwardly, you are not fully able to optimize opportunities. Your gift could carry you where your character won't keep you! In the late 1980s a brilliant financier named Michael Milken was indicted on racketeering and securities fraud charges. Milken was sentenced to ten years in prison, fined $600 million, and was permanently barred from the securities industry by the Securities and Exchange Commission. At that time in his life, Milken had the gift for making money, but not the character. After serving two years in prison and surviving a bout with prostate cancer, Milken took a different direction. He is still gifted at making money and is listed among the top five hundred richest people in the world. He established a family foundation and has devoted a significant amount of his time and fortune to helping others.

3. **Physical reset.** It takes strength to live in your destiny. If you're tired, lack energy, and can't maintain the pace of champions, maybe your lifestyle is unhealthy. Train to triumph! This may be the time to reset how you feed the body you need to perform for you when the opportunities come. Though the most important thing is how you feel, how you look does affect the way people perceive you and relate to you. People take note when your skin does not look healthy because of a poor diet. They watch you move with greater difficulty after you've gained weight. When you look your best, you feel better about yourself, and it shows in the way you walk and the way you present yourself to the world each day.

4. **Emotional reset.** Manage the emotions that historically have managed you. Not falling easy prey to emotional slumps and pitfalls is critical to living your destiny. Unresolved and untreated emotional disease is widespread. If you need counseling, get it. If you need courage to get therapy, find it. But don't allow unhealthy emotions to go unchecked.

5. **Relax to reset.** If you live in a high-stress environment, as I do, you need to know how to take care of you for the long haul. Downtime isn't a waste of time. Rest is as different from laziness as strategy is from manipulation. Rest rejuvenates while laziness deteriorates. Your body's cells need rest to rebuild themselves and fortify you for another day of challenges. Finding ways to distance from your norm and detox is important. It doesn't require an expensive vacation. Find ways to rest your body and mind from day-to-day stress. A walk in the park, a visit to Aunt Sadie's, a weekend camping trip, or even a night at the movies can be highly restorative.

Stay Strong in the Struggle

We've become familiar with the concept of reset largely through our use of electronic devices. Resetting a mobile phone or tablet is usually as quick and simple as pushing a button. It's not so easy to reset a life. Some of us encounter great difficulty trying to reset our lives to steer us properly toward Destiny. The transformation process can be overwhelming. If we're not careful, we can be overtaken by the constant wave of challenges to our efforts to turn our lives around.

A high percentage of drownings occur in shallow water, among experienced swimmers. It seems like it would be simple enough to just stand up in shallow water if you are about to drown, but an amazing number of people drown each year from a condition known as shallow water blackout. It seems strange that you could drown in shallow water, especially after you have survived the deep. It is incongruent to think that you can be overtaken in something you could master. An experienced swimmer doesn't expect to drown in shallow water.

After we've hit a life reset button, things begin to change—some for the better and some seemingly for the worse. Imagine that your life is a song that you dance to. Then you decide to change the music. That means you have to change how you dance and move. You may not always be able to quickly adjust your steps to match the new beat. Sometimes our problems don't arise from the circumstances we predicted, the people we imagined, or the places we calculated. No matter how much you try to plan for trouble, you can never predict how long you will have to do battle or how hard.

Most people know that skirmishes are just part of life's journey, but that doesn't make the trip any easier. It's a great challenge to hold on to your strength during those hard times. You can wrestle with challenges for so long to reach your dreams that you begin to wonder if Destiny is worth what you're having to endure. You feel like giving up, not because the goal isn't worth fighting for; you're just tired of wrangling with problems and issues. Nevertheless, day after day you scramble on, hoping finally to catch a glimpse of that light at the end of Destiny's tunnel.

The struggle may go on much, much longer than you could ever imagine. By the time you get to the end of the fight you can barely hold on. You wonder if you're crazy for holding on. You've been battling so long that you're worn out. You hope for a stroke of luck. You pray for a bit of divine favor. You look for encouragement and search for compassion and understanding; but mostly, you look for relief. When you're deep in battle, what you need is strength to keep going, even when it looks like nothing is going to happen.

The toughest times are not at the beginning of a struggle. The beginning of a battle catches you fresh. You're vibrant and energized. You're cocked and ready for a fight. You adopt a "Bring it on!" attitude, knowing you can win. You're able to put all your energy into the fight because you're determined to beat whatever confronts you.

And you can do it in the beginning. When you find out an extramarital affair is tearing up your marriage, you're ready to fight! You're determined to hold on to your spouse and your family. You're dangerous even. When you hit a rough spot in your small business, you're ready to fight to save the company you worked so hard to build. You're willing to go to the mat!

But what do you do when the struggle seems to have more tenacity than you? How do you stay strong against what seems stronger than you? How do you keep the mental, emotional, and physical stamina to wrestle with fate until it swings favorably in your direction? When you are closest to the shore is when you're closest to collapsing.

Florence Chadwick was a champion swimmer. In 1952, she attempted to swim a span of the peaceful Pacific Ocean between California's Catalina Island and the state coastline. As she began the twenty-six-mile journey, she was accompanied by small boats of supporters who watched for sharks and were prepared to help Florence if she got hurt or grew tired. Thick fog rolled in after about fifteen hours of swimming.

Florence recalled that after already having spent so many hours navigating the waters with her body, she began to doubt her ability. She didn't think she could make it, but she kept going. She swam for another hour before asking to be pulled out, physically and emotionally exhausted. She was tired and in her mind the California coastline felt like it was a million miles away.

After she got into the boat, she learned she had stopped less than a mile short of her destination. She couldn't see the shoreline and the journey began to feel impossible. "All I could see was the fog," she would tell news reporters the next day. "I think if I could have seen the shore, I would have made it."

When it seems like we are so far away from our destination, we want to quit. That's the time to dig in our heels and keep on in the struggle. Don't get into the boat and stop short of your intended destination! You likely are closer than you could ever imagine. Keep seeing the destination in your mind so it will give you the strength to relentlessly move toward it, despite the tiredness, despite the aches, despite the feeling of wanting to give up.

Two months after Florence's failed attempt, she tried again to swim from the California coastline to Catalina Island. During the journey, the same thick fog set in, but this time she succeeded in reaching the shore. This time, she knew she had to keep her destination in sight. The second time, Florence was victorious because she kept a mental image of the shoreline in her mind as she swam. She didn't forget where she was going and it gave her the strength to keep on until she reached her destination.

When you are in the struggle, keep your destination in sight. If your goal is a better life for your children, take a moment to watch them as they sleep peacefully during the night because they trust you to take care of them. If your goal is physical fitness, keep that image of yourself in good health and at goal body weight. Look at old photos of yourself and know that you can be at your goal weight. If it's the corner office at the company, take a photo and post it where you will look at it often.

Keep your destination in sight and keep going. You may be closer than you think. You're aching, but keep going. Even though you're bruised and feel beaten up, keep going. You may feel like you're slowly shutting down, but find the strength to keep going! Never give up. Your next attempt may be the one that takes you over the top on your way to Destiny. Your next business presentation may get you that multimillion-dollar contract. Your attendance at the next social function that you hate going to may be the place where you meet your spouse. Your next job interview may be the one where you hear, "You're hired!"

You Will Make It through the Storm

There are all kinds of storms—physical, financial, emotional, relational, vocational, familial, and the like. Your whirlwind doesn't care that the rest of your life must go on. Emotional, mental, financial, professional, physical, or spiritual blizzards may come in and may almost succeed in overtaking your life as they attempt to take you down for the count. A cyclone of suffering may move in and attack your health, not caring that you are the sole provider for your household. A hurricane of trouble can overcome your home and make you feel like you're filming an episode of *Teenagers Gone Wild*. Life has all types of disturbances that we have to struggle to overcome.

The toughest storms are those that other people can't see. Undetectable monsoons of distress make people think you haven't been through anything because you get up every morning, take a shower, comb your hair, dress well, and go about your business with a smile that you put on just like your outfit. That's a secret storm. Married people go through secret storms. They may be holding hands in public but at home they argue constantly. A business owner may drive a nice car and live in a great home yet be on the verge of filing for bankruptcy to give her a chance to reorganize the company. While people are celebrating the accomplishments they can see, you may be battling a quiet hurricane they can't see, and you strive with all your might to uphold the image.

Maintaining a certain public persona is important. There's nothing wrong with that. It's reasonable for us to project our best selves in public. You present your best self to the world. And frankly, there are times when it may be detrimental for people to know the struggles you're going through. A real estate broker needs to look prosperous, even if he's having a tough time in the market. Most people would be skeptical to contract a Realtor who pulls up in a hoopty to take them to a showing. Image is important, but trying to maintain that image can break you down if you're in a storm and you don't know how to stay strong.

We value our reputation and our name. We want to fit in with a certain group of people, whatever group that is—a professional group, a social group, a financial group, a religious group, or even a community group. We want our peers and our public to think that everything is going well and that there are no problems. We can continue to show that self until real calamity hits. As a pastor, I've been at the nadir of people's lives when things got so tough they could no longer show only their public face. When real trouble comes, no one has time for a mask or a façade.

There's a level of transparency I've been able to witness in people—from presidents to paupers—because I've been called in to counsel at the most challenging times in their lives. I've counseled some people as they fell apart privately while letting outsiders believe that all was well. A secret storm is a terrible kind of hell on earth. When you go through a visible storm, someone will hand you an umbrella or assist you because they are aware of your suffering. But if no one knows you're in trouble, they assume that how you look on the outside is how you're feeling on the inside.

Secret storms are the internal traumas you endure when someone is jealous of the car you're driving, not realizing that you're two months behind on the payments. You won't announce to everyone that you're struggling to pay the note, so you deal with your anxiety as a private storm. Or the coworkers who are envious of your job promotion don't realize you're under so much pressure in the new position that you can't even sleep at night. So you come to work each day and put on your game face, never revealing the truth about your restless nights.

"If this is my God-given destiny, why am I battling through all these storms?" Don't take a life storm as the absence of God. When people are in a storm, they tend to wonder: Where is God? They think if God were with them, they wouldn't be in a storm and things would go smoothly. The family would not be in turmoil. Bill collectors wouldn't be calling. They ask questions like, "How can God be with me and I have cancer?" "How could God let my child die?" "How could my house be in foreclosure?" When we are in a storm, most of our time is spent trying to figure out how to get out of it. Usually we're so focused on getting out that we can't see straight.

No one can see clearly in a storm. That's why we must walk by faith and not simply by what we can see. The storm is hard, but there's a purpose for the storm. The storm is uncomfortable, but there's a purpose for your discomfort. God has plans for you even in the storm. Just because you are in a storm does not negate the presence of God. When you get through battling the storm, you'll have more wisdom, more tenacity, more power, and more vision to take you forward.

The storm can make you stronger and give you confidence to handle future challenges. It's a part of our growing process. Parents must allow their children to learn how to struggle well and grow strong enough to survive. A young woman who suffered massive injuries from a car accident recalled how her mother allowed her to struggle during her rehabilitation process. "I had to learn how to do everything all over again. I had to learn how to tie my shoes. I remember falling off the couch one day. My mother heard me fall but she never came to help me. I was so angry with her at the time because it took me almost an hour to get myself back on that couch. I later realized that she allowed me to struggle so that I could learn to live independently again."

God will not make you comfortable in your storm, but will be right there with you. God has reserved a place for you in life that is your destiny. That is a divine promise from your Creator. You will arrive at Destiny if you do not give up and you do not succumb to the storm. Don't be so distracted by the storm that you lose awareness of God's presence in the storm.

Are you steering your life based on what you see? Or are you steering your life based on what you believe? Instead of steering in the sensual realm, steer in the faith realm. Before the first streak of lightning flashes, before the thunder rolls, and before you even get wet, get one thing settled: I'm going to make it out of this storm! When you see the dark clouds rolling in and feel the moisture in the air, determine that you are going to come out. You may not have the details or a complete plan to make it out. You may not have the money to make it out. You may not have the social or political connections to make it out. No matter how it's going to happen, resolve in your spirit that you will make it out of that storm!

The most important things in life require struggle. As you battle your storm, look for the people who struggled and made it through. They can help you know you're not alone. They can encourage you to hang in there because the storm won't last forever. They can support you when you feel like you're about to drown under the pressure. They can help you know that if they made it out so can you. Find some people who've struggled in a similar way and made it out. Establish relationships with trusted people who can keep you connected and sane while you're going through your storm. You need people who can provide affirmation that they made it out and that you, too, will see your way past the storm.

Change Your Mind to a New Normal

Once you reset your mind and have cultivated a new normal, you may on rare occasions revert back to old thoughts or behaviors. But do not worry or freak out. Since it's no longer your normal, it won't be a permanent reversion. You might get back in it, but you won't stay in it. A pig and a sheep can fall in the same mud. The pig is defaulted to like the mud because it cools him down and keeps his body temperature from rising too high. But if a sheep finds himself in that same mud, he will say, "I don't belong in this mess!" and set about getting out.

Find out where you belong and determine how to get there.

You may have to first get out of the place where you don't belong. When I lived in West Virginia, I knew a woman who was in a very abusive relationship. Her husband was a big guy, about my size, and she was about a third of his size. He used to beat her mercilessly, but she always went back to him. No matter what we said to her, she would always go back to him.

One day she finally realized, "I don't belong in this mess!" When she changed her mind, she no longer accepted herself as an abused woman. The husband could no longer hold her captive mentally or physically. As long as her mind was enslaved to his abuse, she was captive. The same is true about being captive to debt, ignorance, illiteracy, or whatever terrorizes you.

You may have been through some terrible and degrading circumstances—abuse, job loss, bankruptcy, assault—but you don't have to be captive to those experiences. The first challenge is getting your mind out of there. Once the mind is free, all else becomes possible. Once you get your mind clear, you can see the beautiful person you've become and pursue your destiny.

The mind is a personal war zone between right and wrong, success and struggle, destiny and mediocrity. It doesn't matter how successful you are, the battle is still there. You will always have the challenge of keeping your mind in a new place of normal because there are constantly new situations, new challenges, and new opportunities. If you are not flexible enough to change what's in your head, you can't change your life—losing weight, being faithful in marriage, going after a new job, living honest and true.

Change the mind or you won't change anything else. Are you willing to allow a new truth to be planted in your mind to replace past experiences? Or will you instead be imprisoned to a future of ignorance or weakness or evil or fear?

A changed mind means even if people come at you with the same behavior, you don't respond in the same way you used to.

Growing up, I was the baby of the family. My brother and sister used to tickle me and it made me laugh, so they kept doing it. I would laugh so hard that I couldn't breathe. I didn't like the feeling, but I couldn't get them to stop. Through that experience I found a secret that was more powerful than coercing them to stop tickling me. I changed my mind. Since I couldn't control their tickling, I decided that I would no longer respond to their tickling with laughter. And they stopped. When they could no longer get the desired result, they no longer wanted to tickle me.

That early experience taught me a valuable lifelong lesson about the power of a made-up mind. When you decide that you are not inadequate, the person who always puts you down with negative comments will no longer have power over you. The person who makes you feel inferior or intimidates you will have no impact on your changed mind. You don't have to be anything you don't want. Emotions, feelings, thoughts, or fears are secondary. Change your mind.

CHAPTER 8

Time Flies Even When You're Not Having Fun

Take Steps to Protect Your Priceless Commodity

The sooner you develop a mind-set for Destiny, the more days you will have to devote your gifts to the world. The more efficiently you use time to get to know yourself, the greater your opportunity to make the most of the days you are given on earth. Appreciate the value of time by focusing on what's in front of you, not by lamenting what's behind you.

You've heard the expression "Hindsight is twenty-twenty." At any stage of life, we can look back at who we were and see the gifts or the potential we overlooked in ourselves. We see missed opportunities that we can't go back and reclaim. We see youthful vigor that has waned over the years. Hindsight can fuel feelings of regret when we fail to capitalize on the value of time.

Have you ever said, "I wish I knew then what I know now"? That's a reflection made by a person who realizes the value of time and youth. Children and teens can hardly wait to grow up. Then finally, high school and college years pass and you're working your first job; you get your first apartment. Then age thirty hits and after that, time starts passing more quickly. The years just zoom by. You look back over your life and wonder where the years went.

Time is our most valuable resource because it cannot be reproduced or replicated. Once it's gone, it's gone. You can get more money, even if you file for bankruptcy. You can get another job after you lose one. You can get another car if yours is repossessed. You can get another spouse or another house. You cannot get more time if you lose it or waste it.

You don't want to lament time wasted or lost because you were not in tune with your destiny. Be careful with the gift of time. Don't regret missed opportunities. Be wise enough to know that right now, you are smart enough, attractive enough, and secure enough to walk the trail of Destiny.

German-born theologian and author Joseph Wittig observed that a biography should begin with the person's death, because none of us has control over how we were born, but we all have a great deal to do with the way our lives end. Whatever circumstances we were born into, we can choose how we use our time, make a difference in our lives, and leave our footprint on the annals of time.

Every Day Is a Withdrawal from the Bank of Time

I've never calmly accepted the notion of people stealing from me. I may give it to you, but I never accept any excuse for being robbed. The older I get, I recognize that my most precious commodity that needs protection from thieves and robbers isn't the material goods one would normally protect. Clothes, cars, jewelry, houses, money, or investments are not my most valuable assets. Time is what I have learned to guard and hold precious. I can buy a new watch or a coat or a car if mine gets stolen. But I can't get back my time. It's irreplaceable; therefore, it's priceless.

The value of time accrues interest as it slips away. Our expanded use of technology is a prime example. A sixty-year-old adult who is just now getting into the game of smartphones and computers has a huge learning curve to overcome. Conversely, a sixty-year-old adult who has been using a computer for twenty years has a much less difficult time staying current with technological changes. I struggle to keep up with the new-and-improved world in which we live. Gadgets and gigabytes have taken a bite out of my confidence, as I have to ask my grandchildren how to upload a picture to Instagram or download a document in a new file that I don't have an app for. Time and technology are racing so fast that if my parents were here today, they'd be hard-pressed to complete a transaction in the grocery store! Truthfully, I almost get embarrassed at the market trying to check out!

Imagine a bank credits your account each morning with $86,400. It carries over no balance from day to day. At midnight, the account resets to another $86,400 and deletes whatever part of the previous day's balance you failed to use. There's no guarantee you will ever be given another day with $86,400. What would you do? Draw out every cent, of course!

Each of us has such a bank. Its name is time. Each morning, you awaken with a credit of 86,400 seconds. Every night, what you have failed to use is lost. Time carries over no balance from day to day. Time allows no overdraft and you can't hold on to what you did not use the day before. If you fail to use the day's deposits, the loss is yours. There is no going back. There is no drawing against the "tomorrow." Live in the present on today's deposits.

Time Is Priceless

I watched at my mother's bedside as she passed away. As her breath faded, for every sixty seconds that she remained alive, I realized the value of a minute. Her transitioning helped me understand how many precious seconds of my own life I had allowed doubt and fear to creep in and rob me blind of moments that I would never regain. I can still hear the faint breaths escaping from her fragile lungs every time I find myself parked on the road to Destiny by some triviality that doesn't warrant a rest stop or a decrease in the speed of my life.

Thinking of my mother's death caused me to become much more protective of my time and how I spend it. My mom, who was a teacher, taught me a valuable lesson that I am trying to pass on to you. I have walked the halls of Congress and seen representatives and senators still serving at age eighty and wondered why so many of us buy into the notion that our contributions to life end at sixty-five! Just because you don't do what you used to do doesn't mean you can't contribute anything!

Destiny won't allow us to spend our days aimless and listless, only realizing what we've lost after it's gone. To understand the value of one year, just ask a high school senior who failed a grade. To know the significance of one month, talk to a mother who gave birth to a premature baby. How valuable is an hour? Ask the businessman who had a delayed flight and missed an important business meeting. Every single minute is priceless. If you don't think so, just ask the man who had a heart attack and the emergency medical team arrived in the nick of time to save his life. You can't underestimate the value of even a second. Just ask the person who barely missed a head-on collision with an oncoming car. Even a millisecond can change your life, like it would for an Olympic hopeful who missed qualifying by six-tenths of a second.

Mind Your Own Busy-ness

Most of us feel there is never enough time, that there are too many things pulling at us. Why do we feel there isn't time to accomplish our destiny? The issue is not time or that you are busy, but whether the actions and activities that consume your time are leading to your destiny. Or are they the priorities of others who want you to further their agenda? Are you spending time doing what actually hinders your ability to get where you want to be?

It's easy to let someone else's interests control your life. Their agenda can consume your time. Don't spend your time on activities that have nothing to do with your destiny. Don't get bogged down in what fulfills everyone else's needs but your own. You don't have time to pursue anybody else's course to Destiny. It will take all of your time to stay on your own track.

Yes, share your time, but don't invest more in others than in yourself. People who give of themselves can wrongly believe that Destiny is for everyone but them. They encourage everyone but themselves. They push others but never focus on themselves. Living through others is not Destiny.

Beware of the Fast Pursuit of Destiny

When we see a speed demon zipping down the road, we move out of the way, because we know they crash. Some are traveling their life's path with great speed. Everything has to happen quickly. They're going to get where they're going fast. They've got to move ahead of everyone. They don't have time for anything going on around them because they're trying to get someplace right away. You may even envy their quick success.

Then somewhere down the road, they crash. Sometimes from addiction; perhaps from public scandal and there's no Olivia Pope to save them; sometimes from getting everything they wanted, only to be miserable. Sometimes the challenges and difficulties are what cause us to know the value of what we have accomplished.

Our culture values quickness. We want the fastest Internet speed for our computer. We have become accustomed to getting our meals quickly from fast-food restaurants. We prize fast cars. Institutes specialize in distance learning, promoting how quickly you can get an education. Lenders advertise instant loans obtained by phone or online. Our obsession with all things fast makes us want to put our destiny on a stopwatch, too. Destiny cannot and will not be rushed.

Our fast-paced culture can cause us to become frustrated with Destiny's process. Jentezen Franklin, my colleague in ministry, observed, "We are a microwave generation serving a Crock-Pot God." Destiny's pace does not quicken because we are in a hurry. Trust God that there is a reason for delays and seeming setbacks. God is slowly blending ingredients in the Crock-Pot of your life, allowing the flavors to simmer and blend. That slow, creative process cannot happen in a microwave oven. A microwave is a convenient appliance, but it was never meant to replace a conventional oven.

Some things simply take time. Cakes, pot roasts, and turkeys are best served when they have been prepared slowly, with attention to detail of all the ingredients needed. A rush cooking just doesn't produce the best meal. Likewise, a fast-track career can be successful, but there's no cheating time and experience. A person who has a fast ride to success will hit some really hard bumps along the way. The slower journey allows time for maturity and experience to shape you into the person who comfortably fits into your destiny.

Destiny's process is establishing your foundation, creating a stronger you who has the ability to endure everything your destiny demands. There is a plan for your life. That it unfolds slowly—rather than magically appearing in an instantaneous puff of smoke—can, however, be frustrating and discouraging.

Savor Every Moment in Time

If you took a cross-country road trip from the East Coast to the West Coast and could see only the highway that lay ahead, you would miss all the scenery, vast landscapes, changing climate conditions, and people along the way. You would not experience the Southern charm of the friendly gas station attendant, beautiful rows of agriculture as you travel through the Midwest, bright lights of the desert oasis Las Vegas, or the national landmarks along the route. You would get to your destination, but you wouldn't know anything about getting there. You would be glad to arrive at your destination, but wouldn't the journey have been much richer had you experienced what you only passed to get there? Do not be so consumed with reaching your destiny that you ignore that Destiny is a process. The journey to Destiny is just as purposeful as what you accomplish when you get where you want to be. Mistakes, regrets, victories, and people you meet—all are part of your magnificent journey.

When President Obama took his second oath of office, before leaving the platform and ascending the few steps to disappear into the canopied corridor of the US Capitol, he turned and paused to take one last, long look at the tens of thousands of Americans who had gathered on that cold January day to witness his second inaugural ceremony. He knew he would never again stand in that spot as president of the United States. It was a moment I'm sure he wanted to savor.

We can be so busily engaged in the process of Destiny that we forget to take the time to savor special, even ordinary, moments. We discover only in hindsight how much more we might have gleaned from those moments if only we had been paying attention. We start to realize what we missed when a strange-looking boy comes to the front door to date the little girl in pigtails who used to cling to her mother's leg. The boy who loved playing with Ninja Turtles is now only interested in getting his allowance and the keys to your car. From your corner office you see a newly hired employee—a young college graduate full of idealism and determination to challenge the system—trotting off to lunch with colleagues and you smile, because that was once you. You may hear a song on your favorite oldies station that reminds you of your college days and the carefree times you shared with roommates and classmates.

As you prepare for your destiny tomorrow, take the time to savor your journey to Destiny, your today. Enjoy the times of your life, even the bumpy moments. Take pleasure in now, with all of its challenges. You will not have a perfectly smooth journey to the life you desire. Upsets, setbacks, and outright failures will be sprinkled in with what will inevitably seem like too few successes. But savor your life for what it is now.

Treasure every moment that you have! Heed the wise words of cartoonist Bil Keane: "Yesterday is history. Tomorrow is a mystery. Today is a gift. That's why it's called the present!"

Destiny Doesn't Retire

I saw my dear friend Joyce Meyer teaching from a chair on television the other day and thought, "No matter what malady she may be facing, she is still serving her generation and remaining productive." Talk about a message on faith! Service against all odds is proof positive that faith is not daunted by time!

You and I must value the moments we have on this earth and not allow the inevitable need to change certain methodologies to intimidate us from being productive. For example, most job applications today are completed online, so if your computer skills are poor, you may have a difficult time finding a job. Also, nowadays, some things can only be bought online using a credit or debit card. If you can only pay by cash or check, you may experience anxiety trying to buy on the Internet.

I never want to be like the Bible character Naomi, who had lulled her faith to sleep because she had lost loved ones and was entering into a new season. Naomi had to learn that her assignment had merely changed, not ended! It's important to recognize changed assignments. As we grow older, physical limitations may impose limits on what we hope to accomplish. All we need is the faith and determination to continue despite our challenges.

It's so easy to write off the future once we get to a certain age. I was about forty years old when I visited my aging grandmother and foolishly announced to her that I was getting old! In my mind I was old, as I was the oldest I had ever been! She snickered at my misguided calculation and responded with words I will never forget. She looked at me and smiled. "Tommy, as long as you can get up without planning it for thirty minutes, you are not old!" Grandma taught me in that moment that perspective has everything to do with production! Could it be possible that in order to remain productive, you may need to change your perspective?

We have to pay attention to what's going on around us. If not, we will begin to think that every successful person is younger, smarter, or has more savvy to get ahead.

Truthfully, many older adults are enrolled in college to obtain undergraduate or advanced degrees. More people than ever are taking early retirement incentive packages and leaving corporate or government positions to engage in a different purpose. Often people work jobs that may not be fulfilling or even desirable because they have a family to support or some other type of obligation that commits them to a certain line of work. But when the kids are grown and self-supporting or the aged parent has passed on or the mortgage is paid off, people start looking at life for the things they want to do rather than the things they feel they have to do. Please make every effort not to be the person who grows old and bitter because of lost opportunities while failing to affirm younger people who understand and have seized every valuable moment.

Someone wisely observed, "Today you're the oldest that you've ever been and the youngest that you'll ever be." Time is winding up, not moving backward. You will never go back to the way things used to be. The good old days, which some lament are gone, probably weren't all that great in the first place. People tend to glorify the past, especially when they are struggling with the future. Admittedly, we all are growing older by the millisecond! But just because time continues to move forward is no reason to shrink into unproductivity and allow opportunities to be stolen by your fears. The cool breeze of death warms the heart to maximize the moment.

Sometimes the reality of time lost is the fire that ignites under our feet to get us moving on to new avenues of Destiny. Age is no excuse for a lack of productivity. As long as you awaken each morning, you have more to do. We can take examples from so many people who made significant accomplishments at an age most people mark for retirement. Grandma Moses did not start painting until she was seventy-six. She tried her hand as an artist when her hand became too stiff to crochet.

Satchel Paige became the oldest Major League Baseball player at age fifty-nine when he played for the Kansas City Athletics in 1965. Coco Chanel was the head of her fashion design firm at age eighty-five. Author Laura Ingalls Wilder published her first book at age sixty-four, chronicling her life as a wife and mother, which was the basis for the television series *Little House on the Prairie.*

You can retire from a job, but not from your destiny. Every day you awaken is a sign that you have more to contribute to life. If you didn't, you'd be dead. So stop worrying about what it's too late for you to do and concentrate on the skills you have and how they can make a valuable contribution to society. Maybe you can't accomplish the thing you dreamed of originally, but that's no reason to tuck your destiny in a file cabinet. You can't make it in the NBA at age forty, but you can help train young athletes and remind them to keep their heads on straight amid the accolades of the cheering crowds. You may have passed the time for having a baby of your own, but you can still adopt or mentor children through a respected community program. The aging process may give you the wisdom and exposure you need to engage in a project or task you never envisioned.

Remember the saying that age is just a number. It's important to respect time as a valuable commodity, but it's even more important to savor whatever time you have left to maximize each moment for Destiny.

Take Your Eyes Off the Clock

As valuable as time is, you don't have to be crippled by feeling you have lost time. You may have missed many opportunities and feel like you've gotten so far off track in your life that Destiny seems impossible. As you look at the accomplishments of others, it may seem like they have traveled the superhighway of success while you have been consigned to the scenic route, and the view ain't looking too good.

Most people are not happy with what they have accomplished over the span of their life. If you became a millionaire by age fifty, you may feel inadequate because you're comparing yourself to someone who became a millionaire by age twenty-one. If you earned a PhD by age forty, you may feel inadequate because so many others finished before the age of thirty. When you focus on doing you, you can appreciate the accomplishments you've made, even though achieving them took longer than you planned.

Doing you may mean it takes you longer to succeed at something than it does someone else. If you're thinking you're too old to achieve your dream, ask yourself how old you will become if you give up the pursuit. Time is important; it's critical. But don't let the passage of time be your excuse for not pursuing Destiny. You still have purpose.

Looking at the clock to judge your accomplishments can make you want to give up. Keep pushing. Your delays may have given you experience and wisdom that will propel you to the place you are supposed to be. Your setbacks may have given you the maturity to know how to focus on what is important. Your disappointments may have set you up to seize and truly appreciate future opportunities.

God's time is not ours. We don't add up time the same way God does, so don't try. You'll only frustrate yourself. Since time is in the Almighty's hands, God can use every day you have left to complete the task you have been called to fulfill. Time is too precious to waste, but time is not the determining factor in your destiny. That is a partnership between you and your Creator.

Don't Die in Your Nest

In Chapter Three, I discussed eagles. A mother eagle gets her eaglets out of the nest and lets them learn to fly. The day comes when every person must leave the security of the nest and pursue their destiny.

However, I've known people who never come out of their nest. They always have an excuse for why they haven't accomplished anything or why they've been hindered from fulfilling a dream.

Don't die in your nest. Get out and live the life God has intended for you. Only you can live it. God needs you to live it. You need you to live it.

Ours is an interesting culture where everyone wants to live a long time but nobody wants to be old. Longevity, however, should not be our primary life purpose. It's easy to live a long life, at least in America. Look at the United States Department of Health and Human Services statistics: out of every hundred thousand persons, 94 percent reach fifty years of age, more than 77 percent make it to seventy, and almost 40 percent get to eighty-five or more. Lots of people live a long time, but the important thing is what they do with that time. Rather, we should be concerned with giving significance and value to all our years.

Most of the products we buy at the grocery store have expiration dates. Anyone who has ever had a glass of milk after the date on the container knows it's important to pay attention to the date stamped on the package. None of us knows our life expiration date, but we all can be certain that it is coming. Since we know this is true, how should we approach the days God has given us? How many days have you lived, and what have you done with those days?

Young Ruby Bridges was chosen at age six to integrate New Orleans's elementary schools. She had lived only about 2,200 days before showing the world the faith of a child as she marched innocently to school amid racist chants. Anne Frank lived only about 5,700 days, but the diary she wrote about her days in isolation during World War II would touch the world. Martin Luther King lived only about 14,300 days. But he changed history during his thirty-nine years.

Our lives are a series of days, one after another. Each day is an opportunity to either seize Destiny's invitation or pass it by.

CHAPTER 9

Keep the Destiny Vision

Connect Where You Came from to Where You're Going

Mr. Smith goes to heaven. St. Peter is stationed at the pearly gates to take heaven's newest resident on a tour. The two walk together, viewing all the glories of heaven: the streets paved with gold, the palatial houses of the faithful. The man notices a warehouse that doesn't fit in the heavenly scenery. The building has no windows, only one door.

"What is inside the building?" he asks.

St. Peter hesitates to respond. "You really don't want to see inside there."

Mr. Smith wonders, "Why would there be secrets in heaven? There must be something awfully special in there." He pleads to see inside the building.

Finally Peter relents. "Okay, Mr. Smith, but remember that I told you that you really don't want to see what's inside."

The door opens and Mr. Smith rushes inside. To his delight the cavernous structure is filled with row after row of shelves, each neatly stacked floor to ceiling with beautiful boxes tied in red ribbons. Each box has a name on it.

"Do I have one of these?" Mr. Smith asks St. Peter.

"Yes, you do," St. Peter replies as he tries to guide Mr. Smith back outside. But Mr. Smith sprints to the *S* section and finds the box with his name on it. As St. Peter catches up, Mr. Smith is slipping the red ribbon from his box and lifting the lid. He looks inside and instantly recognizes the contents. He releases a deep sigh of regret. St. Peter has heard this sigh countless times. Inside the box are all the gifts God wanted to give Mr. Smith while he was on earth, but unfortunately, Mr. Smith had never tried to use the gifts he received, so God could not give him more.

Don't leave your God-given gifts unopened. Don't leave this planet having missed the great opportunities God has for you. Rip off the lid of your abilities, tear into that box that is your talents, and use every gift God has given you. Devote yourself to fulfilling the unique purpose that is your destiny.

Run the Race with Blinders On

Few things are more beautiful than the grace, form, and style of a racehorse in competition. In addition to all the years of planning, training, and grooming, a horse race relies on a small but critical apparatus: the horse's headgear. This essential piece of equipment makes all the difference in the race. Blinkers block the racehorse's rear and side vision, forcing him to focus only in a forward direction. Racehorses need blinders, or blinkers as they are known professionally, to keep them from getting off track during the race.

What if you could don a set of blinkers to keep you focused on Destiny and undistracted by the circumstances around you? What if blinkers could help you ignore the criticism of people who don't think you're doing a good enough job, although you're giving it your best? Blinkers could help you forget the past that you need to leave behind. Wouldn't Destiny be so much simpler if we could wear headgear to help us ignore what doesn't matter?

If there *was* such a device, you would lose the benefits to having full vision. Peripheral vision prevents you from getting blindsided. You must be able to look back to know what not to return to. You need the ability to see if anything is approaching you from behind.

But you can develop the capacity to wear helpful mental blinkers.

When horses race, they are close together, so it is essential that they not pay attention to what the horses to the right and left are doing. Each horse's ability to finish the race depends on his focus on the track ahead. Learn the art of wearing mental blinkers so you are not easily distracted by someone else's race. Your best friend from high school already has a master's degree, and you're just getting back in school to finish your undergraduate studies. Your neighbor just bought a big luxury car, and you're driving Old Reliable that's paid off so you can afford to pay down your credit card debt. All your girlfriends have gotten married, and you're the only single one left. You're stymied from reaching your destiny because you're too worried about what other people are saying about you, consumed with who has more money in the bank, a bigger house, more education, or the most prestigious career. Put on your blinkers. Your mental blinkers will keep you from being distracted by convention and fear and stagnation. Distractions destroy Destiny.

Someone else's journey has nothing to do with yours! When your own journey is not taking the straight course you'd like, it's easy to focus on what someone else is doing. Cultivate the ability to stay on track—your track—and keep moving forward.

Certainly, you can pay attention to another person's journey to gain insight or inspiration, but do not become competitive. Focus on where you're headed. As the Wizard of Oz told Dorothy and her crew, "Pay no attention to that man behind the curtain!" Don't spend your time obsessing about what others are doing. Traveling your own path to Destiny is all-consuming.

Your mental blinkers can also help you ignore the counterproductive thoughts and feelings going on inside you when the path gets hard and rocky. Get your mind right by putting on your blinkers to ignore the feelings of anxiety that can incapacitate you. Your blinkers can help you ignore the insecurities that make you afraid to say, "My work is good enough." Your blinkers can help you shut down the negative message that what you desire is impossible. Your blinkers will keep your vision of Destiny before you so you will continue infusing it with all your energies.

All of these negative speculations are distractions that will weigh you down and get your life out of focus.

Don't obsess about what other people are doing. Your destiny is not living to keep up with the Joneses. What God has for your life is much more exciting than imagining what goes on in anyone else's life. Your path to Destiny is like no one else's. Keep looking ahead and let God's creativity unfold in your life and amaze you.

I was almost grown before I realized that when I was a child, we were poor. All I knew then was that life was good and that my parents loved us. We didn't have a lot of things, but we had love. As I grew older, from time to time I encountered things that let me know we were poor. I remember not knowing what spaghetti sauce was. I didn't know what a meatball was, either. When our mama made spaghetti she poured ketchup on it. The first time I saw real spaghetti sauce, I was leery about eating it. "Why does that spaghetti have stuff in it?" I asked when I saw the green peppers and meatballs and spices in the sauce.

Things like that helped me to know we were poor. But though my mother poured ketchup on the spaghetti we ate, my parents also gave us a glimpse into a way of life beyond what our economic status would allow. They took us to free ballet and symphony performances to expose us to other cultures. They drove us through wealthy neighborhoods so that we could see how other people lived.

Our parents took the time to teach us many things. My father, a janitor who built his own business, talked to us about the business: the importance of paying quarterly income taxes and keeping paperwork in order. And even though I was just a kid who was only interested in playing, the lessons he taught me stayed with me and helped position me to one day become CEO of my own business enterprise.

God has a way of taking the disconnected pieces of your life and bringing them all together to shape your destiny. Whether you grew up poor, middle class, or wealthy, your experiences play a role in your life. Whether you had one parent or both parents or were raised in a foster home, how you grew up matters to your life. Whether you were popular in school or you were the wallflower who was awkward and uncomfortable in social situations, you were affected by that. Nothing you have been through will be wasted. Every element of who you are has brought you to where you are and will continue to influence you on your way to Destiny.

Every person has had some experiences that elicited the question "Why am I going through this?" Why did my father die and leave us destitute? Why was my stepbrother so mean to me? Why did I have cancer as a child? Why did I have to quit college to care for my alcoholic mother? Our difficulties shape our lives, but so do the normal, everyday experiences. Situations that seemed insignificant may have had a greater impact on your life than you ever realized, like running errands for

Miss Ruth, the lady next door. Cutting lawns to earn money when school was out, having a newspaper route, playing basketball, running for homecoming queen, or getting a part-time job flipping burgers are all experiences that can help build us up and shape us for a purpose that is greater than anything we could see at the time.

When you are blessed to operate in Destiny, you can look back on your experiences and see how all of them helped position you. You realize that the situations that looked like delays actually were opportunities to grow, to gain experience, and to meet people who would help you later in life. See how God used all of these events to shape you. Even the things you didn't want, if you allow them, can be building blocks to a stronger, better you.

When Destiny is your focus, you will realize that not one experience you've had, not one lesson you learned, not one heartache you suffered, not one tear you shed is wasted. Don't worry about who didn't raise you, whether Papa was a rolling stone. Let go of who didn't love you if your heart was broken by someone who pretended to care. If you open yourself to them, these things can be used to build you up, not tear you down. Learn to look differently at everything you've been through and give up the victim mentality. God will use all your experiences to fortify you with wisdom and knowledge to fulfill your destiny.

Why does God do it that way? Why didn't God just equip you with what you need without putting you through all of that? The answer is pretty simple. You cannot bring people where you have not been. God allows you to experience some things, and then brings you through them so that you can help others because of what you've been through. How can you lead others to a place you are still wishing for or have never been? The best education you receive to equip you for Destiny will not come from a classroom, not even in prestigious institutions like

Harvard or Howard or Vassar or Morehouse. It will come from the trials and difficulties that you go through. Every experience, good or bad, has shaped you into the person you are today. God wouldn't have brought you through it if there were nothing more for you to aspire to.

You are the sum total of your experiences, and each round should take you into the next dimension. Your strength should build from one situation to the next. When you have your first scare as a business owner, you feel like everything will cave in on you. But it prepares you for the next episode. When you make it through, you learn that God is able to send people and resources to you that you never imagined. Then the next challenge comes. This time, you're not devastated or immobilized because this ain't your first time at the rodeo. You're able to keep your calm as you work diligently. You can encourage your employees to remain hopeful as you work together and stay strong through your latest business challenge.

Each experience, each challenge, each lesson will take you to the next dimension, building on what's already inside you. Whether you know it or not, God's been prepping you for Destiny before you were even aware that you had a destiny. God has been preparing you for what you are about to do all of your life. You have had no wasted experiences.

Destiny Requires Street Cred

God lets you go through challenges to give you credibility in a certain area and the ability to help someone else out of a situation that you once were in.

How could you possibly encourage me that I will make it through a bankruptcy if you've been wealthy and privileged all of your life? You need street cred to talk to me. You need to be able to tell me how you couldn't get a car loan and had to bum a ride to get to work until things got better. How can you tell me how to help raise my children in the ghetto if your children grew up in the Hamptons? You need street cred to talk to me about how you were a teenage father who worked at McDonald's while you finished high school to help take care of your child.

I spoke to a group of young pastors who were very frustrated that their ministries weren't progressing as quickly as they anticipated. I told them that you have to earn the right to be heard. People won't just follow you because you say so. They will only follow you when you have endured, developed, grown, and sometimes suffered. That's not just true of pastors. Every leader must have the credibility to lead through experience. You can't be healed without having had an illness, lifted from poverty without experiencing destitution, or delivered without ever having been ensnared.

Avoiding the process doesn't create the promise; instead, it is the gateway to problems. What matters most is not found in the destination but is revealed in the issues that we have to resolve along the way to Destiny. The Bible rightly says that experience brings about patience, and patience brings forth hope. This isn't simply a matter of a degree. It isn't about a trophy. It is the hard work of training, rehearsals, failure, and rebounding over and over again.

I had an opportunity to address a group of students who had been selected for Fox News's prestigious Ailes Apprentice Program. The visionary of the program, Fox News chairman and CEO Roger Ailes, shared that he started the mentorship program to introduce more minorities to the field of journalism. He understands that the gap isn't closed by degrees alone, but also by inclusion and access to the relationships that lead to discovery and promotion. He realized that although many minorities have earned degrees, they typically don't have relationships inside the media to get the hand up that is often needed to move a résumé from the bottom to the top of the pile, or to nail down a job.

Education is not enough for people who have historically and systemically been excluded and denied access. Although you can have a degree, what is needed to achieve maximum success is hands-on experience in an environment that extends beyond textbooks. An opportunity to move from the classroom to the world of trials and tests that come in a real work environment. If your parents didn't come from that world, you have a much harder time getting a foot in the door or breaking through a glass ceiling. Ailes's idea was to provide a mentorship program for minority students to gain access and build contacts while being paid. I walked away from that event with a confirmation that education doesn't trump experience!

Street cred is hard won and Destiny requires you to pay it forward. God helps you through hard times so you can help someone else. If you were able to get off drugs but walk around today like you don't even know what drugs are, you're not helping anybody. Even if you work every day, pay your taxes, go to church, and serve in community organizations, if you're not using what you've been through to encourage somebody else, you're not helping anybody. Tell people how you collected aluminum cans to pay your rent, or how you worked three jobs while you put yourself through college, or how you took care of two aging parents while you raised two children. Somebody else is going through that same situation, and they need to see you so that they can see what life looks like on the other side of trouble.

It's Complicated

Very few people grow up with two parents, two siblings, a dog, a cat, and a couple of goldfish in a neatly built house with a well-manicured lawn in the suburbs. For most of us, there are details that make our life story complicated. You can't tell but half the story of how you were raised, because it's complicated. You had no say in the circumstances into which you were born or the way you were reared. You can't explain to people that you were born in a prison infirmary because your mother was locked up on a burglary charge when she gave birth to you, so it's complicated. People won't understand that your mama's boyfriend was married to someone else, but he was the only father figure you ever knew. It's complicated. People might shy away from you if you tell them your brother served time for shooting your father to keep him from beating your mother. It's complicated. Your grandparents raised you because your parents were both addicted to drugs. It's complicated. Your parents were well respected in the community and you all looked like the ideal family, but your father and mother slept in separate bedrooms and barely spoke to each other at home. It's complicated.

If you look deeper at your life and the uniqueness of its complications, they are the clues that unfold Destiny. Every strange, dysfunctional, or unexplainable event in your life helped make you the person you are. The experiences don't necessarily make sense at the time they're happening, but they shape you. They can affect you and mold you into a person of Destiny.

Some view life's complications as a storage compartment for excuses why they cannot succeed. With every setback, they draw into their past and say things like, "My dad always told me I wasn't very bright."

Learn from your experiences as a single parent, a divorcée, a person who had a lot of haters, a person who struggled on minimum wage, renting a single room in a flop house, and use them as the building blocks for a stronger you.

Any experience you have can make you stronger, not just the

negative ones. Managing a paper route as a child, bagging groceries in high school, being a cheerleader, or selling magazines door-to-door are the kinds of experiences that can also be our training ground for broader responsibilities.

When I was about fourteen, I was choir director at my church. Often we would travel overnight to sing at other churches. Even though I was just a kid, I would have to make sure that everyone got checked in to their hotel room and settled and all the other logistics were handled. God was teaching me responsibility and accountability as a teenager to prepare me to pastor the Potter's House and manage my own business today.

Dig Deeper Inside You

Don't let anything hinder your metamorphosis. Keep on pushing ahead because there is more inside you than what you are right now. Sooner or later, caterpillars turn into butterflies, tadpoles turn into frogs, and eggs turn into chickens. Let your vision of your destiny draw out of you the person you really are. When the appointed time comes, you will transform into the fullness of what you were created to be.

Let your identity be shaped by the power of Destiny because there is more inside you than what you already have conceived. Whatever you have done and whatever you're doing right now do not reflect the totality of your gifts. There are gifts in you that you have not tapped into yet. Even when you think you have exhausted the talents inside you, there are more talents buried down deeper. That's right! You have treasure hidden inside you that you haven't even touched yet. You just may not know how to tap into it yet. You may not know how to pull it out, draw it down, or shake it up, but keep on marching toward Destiny.

What you see right now, what's going on right now, where you are right now—none of those things represent what you're truly capable of. Whether it's the most wonderful time in your life or you're in the pits doesn't matter if you're focused on your destiny. Keep looking toward what's ahead while you draw on the strength of lessons learned from the past. No matter how it might seem outwardly, if you have an inkling of faith in yourself and in your God, declare that there is more inside you yet to be discovered, and focus your attention on getting it.

Don't Say, "Don't Go There!"

Before the days of GPS, I would drive in unfamiliar places and, more often than not, I'd get lost. The crazy thing was that even though there was no GPS, I always had a map with me. It didn't make a lot of sense to spend time roaming aimlessly down unknown streets when there was help available to get me to where I needed to go. Some do that with their lives. They waste time, sometimes years, because they won't take the time to ask for guidance and direction to get to the place they want to be.

Some find it hard to trust God for guidance and direction because they don't know where that will take them. They want to reserve the right to tell God, "Don't go there!" if they fear the Almighty will lead them to a place that's unfamiliar or uncomfortable. Destiny is not for comfort seekers. Destiny is for the daring and determined who are willing to endure some discomfort, delay gratification, and go where Destiny leads.

What do you do when God's will sends you beyond your friends? Is Destiny more important than the people who are claiming to be your friends? A person who truly cares for you wants you to aim for the stars—and reach them, if you can. As you rise toward Destiny, you'll find out who really loves you, cares about you, and wants the best life for you.

Are you willing to endure ridicule? Do you have the dexterity of character, being flexible enough to operate in a spirit of excellence, when you don't know where the experience will take you? You never know where your experiences will lead, so as God guides you, move with a spirit of excellence.

When Destiny calls, be prepared to follow where it leads, even if the place is unfamiliar, intimidating, or uncomfortable. If you stay faithful to it, Destiny will guide you through and you will become so comfortable that you'll feel like you never belonged anyplace else. When you arrive at a place where you were meant to be, you can't imagine another way of life bringing you fulfillment. As it all comes together, you will be able to look back and see the divine orchestration of your journey and be grateful for all of it, the good, the bad, and the ugly, because it took all of that to get you where you were meant to be.

If you're serious about traveling the road to Destiny, keep going, knowing there will be times when God allows you to enter an environment where the odds are against you. God will snatch you out of your comfort zone and out of your element. On your training ground to Destiny, you may be thrust into a situation where you have no leverage. You might be in a place where your family name doesn't mean a thing. You may go to a place where people who drive expensive cars are looked upon with suspicion. The place God sends you may be one that has certain expectations for women to be submissive or docile. You may, for a time, go into a place where the things you are good at are not respected. The good news is that while the road may be twisted and crooked, for every divinely inspired vision there is a provision to get you to it and through it.

Provision for Your Vision

I was invited to preach at various churches in West Virginia, but during that time my car was repossessed. I had to hitch a ride to do the task that I knew without a doubt God had called me to. It would have been great to have my own car, but God gave the provision. It wasn't what I imagined or what I would have chosen, but God made a way for me to get to every preaching engagement. I will always remember those days with gratitude, because God made a way. I can't forget those days when I think about the times when people have simply gifted vehicles to my wife and me just because. I can't forget that God has brought us from needing a car to having more cars than we need. We now have more cars than we have garage space.

When you are faithful to the vision, God makes the provision every step of the way. It doesn't always come in the way you plan, but the provision is there. If the vision is for family, God may lead you to a couple struggling to raise their children, and you broaden your understanding and definition of family, which provides all the love you could have hoped for. Open your mind and heart to God's provisions for Destiny and it will lead you there unfailingly.

Your vision may be down in you in seed form right now. In fact, it may be there for a long time. Trust that God is preparing you and the people around you. God is allowing you to develop relationships you can trust before he blesses you. When he does pour it out, it will be so much you won't know if people are following you for what you have or just for you.

Isn't that exciting to think about? Whatever your God-given Destiny vision is, the Almighty has made provision for it. Be excited about that. Wake up every day with an agenda because you have a purpose! And it's wonderful to know that the provisions for your vision extend far beyond financial resources. In your pursuit of Destiny, God provides in many ways.

You've got a great Provider backing you, so expect something significant in your life. Everybody's not going to have a worldwide ministry. If you have a vision, you will have the provision along the way. Learn to recognize seed-form blessings, as discussed in the section in Chapter One titled "First Draw Internally." Your seed to achieve comes from the divine thoughtfulness of God, who has prewired you to find the provision for your vision.

You can wish, hope, and pray for a provision, but you need a vision for it. If you're praying for a job but you don't know why anyone would want to hire you, it's going to be hard to get hired. See yourself as the person who is destined to do that job. You can ask for a spouse, but if you don't see why anyone would want to marry you, you may never marry. See the desirable person that you are, the person who would be an enhancement to your spouse's life. See the wonderful characteristics in you that would attract someone to you and inspire them to want to get to know you better and spend a lifetime with you.

A clear vision steers you to the provision you need for Destiny.

Understand the Complexity of Destiny

When we envision our destiny, we imagine success, fame, financial increase, material abundance, and a position of power and influence. Your destiny may include all of those, but it also will include the challenges of getting there.

Nelson Mandela was a principal figure in dismantling South Africa's system of apartheid, later became the nation's president, and was an influential world leader. That was his destiny. But his destiny also included twenty-seven years in prison, of which eighteen involved hard labor and the harshest conditions. His destiny included being beaten and humiliated. His destiny included the harm his activism brought to his family, and he wondered whether it was worth the cost. Nelson Mandela's reputation as a world power cannot be embraced without his years of prison and sacrifice of his family.

The complexity of Destiny means accepting the difficult side of your purpose in life. Mrs. King understood and accepted the vicissitudes of her role as the wife of a controversial black leader. Like her, like Mandela, we must face the challenging aspects of our destiny, the highs and lows, joys and sorrows, gains and sacrifices.

The young people who became known as Freedom Riders in the 1960s were destined to be beaten and arrested so that generations after them could enjoy equal access to public accommodations. The men and women who were viciously attacked as they marched across Selma's Edmund Pettus Bridge were destined to play a role in fast-forwarding the passage of our nation's Voting Rights Act of 1965. No matter how difficult, no matter how it looks to the world, fulfillment will only come through following the hard places where Destiny leads.

As you follow your instinct to connect to your purpose, understand that challenges pave the way to Destiny. The business cash flow issues are a part of your destiny. The marital challenges are a part of your destiny. Even the tragedies.

You may be going through a challenging time and begin to feel your life has no purpose because of your troubles. Nothing could be further from true! Your challenges are part of the road to Destiny. Let the difficulties teach you endurance, strengthen you, and challenge you to keep going. You're most tempted to give up when you're in the midst of trouble. But remind yourself that the challenge is part of your destiny. You can't predict where it's going to lead.

As Nelson Mandela served his life sentence doing hard labor in the limestone quarry at South Africa's Robben Island, he could not have imagined that he would one day be president of the same nation that had convicted him of treason. His boat trip to the prison island where he was sentenced to spend his life was a stop on Destiny's path that eventually led him to his country's highest office.

Don't Stay at the Party Too Long

Have you ever hosted a social event at your home and had a guest who did not have sufficient perceptiveness to figure out it was time to leave? You've started putting away the food. The music has been turned off. Everyone else, except the people who live there, has already gone. You try to be polite because you don't want to scream, "Get out!" You throw hints about being sleepy. You talk about having to get up early the next morning, but the person refuses to leave. You may actually have to tell them it's time to go home. And more likely than not, you won't invite that person to your home again.

Just like your party wasn't meant to go on forever, some provisions for your vision are not meant to stay in your life forever. But you may be tempted to hold on to them. Be willing to release a provision that has reached its end. Letting go is especially hard for some people, particularly fearful people. Holding on to a temporary provision can block you from a greater provision you need to get to the next level. There's a stage where you need to switch because everything was not meant to last forever.

We hang on to things—people, relationships, jobs, houses—because we are afraid that nothing else will come along. As long as you are afraid of letting go of something because you fear nothing else will come along, you will hold on to a temporary blessing too long and you have to be forced out. God can use many channels to bless you. But the manner of provision can change. Don't limit your thinking with tunnel vision. When Destiny is calling, you may get kicked out of the small place you are in to be received into a larger place.

You will have lots of experiences on the road to Destiny, and many of them may feel like a waste because in the moment, from day to day, you can't see that God is making provision for your vision. It happens in small increments. Stay focused and faithful because one by one those increments add up until you come into the fullness of who you are meant to be.

If you are truly a child of Destiny, determined, don't give up. You really are closer than you think. Stay faithful to Destiny each step of the way. You don't know which day will be *that* day. One phone call, one meeting, one random encounter can change your life. Let all of your decisions and actions be guided by the fact that you may be right on the edge of Destiny.

Problems always hit hardest when you're almost there. Trouble is not a sign that you are far away. No, calamity strikes because you're almost there.

The most dangerous thing that can happen on the road to Destiny is a loss of vision. Firmly fix your mental perception, your vision of yourself, and conceive the invisible. You are standing on the cusp of your vision. If you conceive the invisible you can do the impossible.

You are closer to Destiny than ever, wiser than you have ever been, because you've learned from the ups and downs you have experienced. You are stronger than you've ever been because you have endured hardship, hurt, and betrayal of false friends, and are still standing. You are closer than ever because you've figured out who you are and who you are not. You know what you want and where you belong. You have let go of the people and the circumstances that have no role in your future. You're closer than ever because you live in ever-growing awareness of what matters in your life and what does not. Smell and taste your destiny. You know you are close because you are striving. Soon the entire unfolded journey will make sense.

CHAPTER 10

Put a Stop to What's Stopping You

Step Out of Stuck!

Everybody has felt trapped in a situation they've outgrown. Those who are in step with Destiny cannot wait for others to see their hidden potential and cause a breakthrough. It's time for you to move if you feel confined, suffocated, or frustrated. If everything inside you awaits the opportunity to break out but you're exasperated because there's no opportunity, big break, or anything you can do to move out of this rut, prepare to strategize.

When you stay in a situation for an extended period, you can feel trapped. You can be stymied by your career, relationships, finances, educational level, emotions, past, physical abilities, or even routines of life. You long to take even the tiniest step but moving requires an openness to stretch beyond your comfort zone and out of the familiar.

If you've got an appointment with Destiny, you will have to

move. Destiny can make way for circumstances to shake you loose to help you get unstuck.

"Bishop, I'm ready for a change," you may be thinking. "I'm ready for God to shake things up so I can get unstuck!"

Be careful what you pray for, because you just might get it. Make sure you're ready for the ride! The process of getting unstuck may not be the joyful ride you planned, especially if you're a creature of habit or one who gravitates to the familiar. I am a loyalist to the familiar. If you are my friend, you're my friend. If I'm connected to you, it doesn't matter if you're in deep or hot water, I'm in there with you, rowboat or not, life vest or not. As a result, I have been stuck in friendships that I needed to extricate myself from, and it was painful.

God may have to shake you to get you unstuck and on the right path. And people who persecute you actually can be agents for positive change. That means you may have to get fired to get unstuck. It may mean God will use the divorce you fought against to get you unstuck. God may use a health scare to get you unstuck from unhealthy eating and lack of exercise. The slammed door may cause you to turn and look in another direction for the door that's open and waiting for you to enter. What you cried about in the moment actually can become your blessing.

You've Already Got It Going On, Baby!

What do you do to get unstuck? First, take a good look at your life. You probably have more going on than you realize. Your life may be different from what you perceive. You may be a success and not know it, because you don't have to feel successful to be successful. Distinguish how or where you are stuck and what needs to move from what adds stability and normalcy to your life. Don't start messing with things in your life that don't need to be messed with right now. Maybe it's *not* your marriage that's stuck, not your children, not your job, not your house, not your college major. Work with what you have and build on that.

A story I read illustrates this point well. A donkey fell into an abandoned well. The farmer who owned him paced frantically as he tried to figure out how to get the donkey out. His neighbors convinced him that the donkey was too old to worry about, that it was most humane to bury him alive. They each got a shovel and began to toss dirt into the well. The donkey wailed as he realized he was about to be buried alive, but, instinctively, each time a shovel of dirt fell on his back he shook it off. Then the donkey stopped whining and kept shaking off each shovel of dirt. As the dirt fell under his feet, the donkey stomped on it, which made it turn hard. When the farmer mustered the courage to look down in the well for one last look at his old companion, he was amazed! He watched the donkey as he shook off every load of dirt that hit his back. With each new load, the donkey would shake it off and take a step up on the new layer of dirt. It wasn't long before the donkey stepped up over the edge of the well and trotted off, to the astonishment of the farmer and all of his neighbors. Whatever you have going on for you right now should not bury you; instead, use it as a steppingstone to raise you to the next level.

From Stuck to Strategy

Getting unstuck will mean leaving behind some behaviors or beliefs and cultivating new relationships and experiences. A woman who worked with an organization whose mission was to produce more professionals from the inner city explained,

"Bishop, I work with people who fought their way up from the streets to get a degree and a job, but many times they can't maintain employment because under pressure, they rely on old methodologies." Instead of handling corporate disputes according to corporate America's rules, they would revert to what was familiar—the rules of the streets.

All people have a tendency to revert back to the familiar when under pressure. A Southerner can speak without a drawl, except when under pressure. A person from another country may revert to his native language when under pressure. An alcoholic may forsake years of recovery and take a drink when under pressure. You can stay stuck in a situation because you rely on the methods of where you have been, rather than crafting a new one for where you're going.

Dependence on old, familiar ways can't be fixed by anything outside you. Getting more education won't fix that dependence. Buying a new house in a gated community won't fix that. Marrying a new spouse won't fix that. Driving a big luxury car won't fix that. You can change jobs, houses, spouses, or even cities, when what really needs to change is you.

You will stay stuck on stuck if you respond to a 2015 situation with a 1989 approach. Remember what mobile phones looked like in 1989? The few people who had them needed a carrying case to cart them around. They really were car phones, because it wasn't practical to carry those big, heavy things around. And they were expensive. Most phones then cost far more than the average family's budget could afford. They were the tools and toys of physicians and corporate types who needed continuous access. You couldn't use that phone today. That old analog equipment would not match the digital technology of today. You'd be stuck if you used a floppy disk to store data in a Google Drive world.

Get in tune with your actions and behaviors that need to

change so you can correctly focus on your destiny. Pinpoint how you can learn to change so you don't mess with relationships and situations that don't need to be messed with. Get unstuck.

When Destiny provides the opportunity for you to get unstuck, heed the signal to change and to take action. Adopt new behavior to get out of your small life. Adapt in order to get out of a stuck place. Get unstuck from the self-imposed constrictions, learned limitations, rigidity, and closed-mindedness. They will only keep you stuck.

Being stuck can only bring you frustration, which is an enemy that will wreck your plan for Destiny. The frustration won't change with a stroke of good luck. It shifts through strategy. Move from stuck to strategy and bring about the change you need in preparation for Destiny.

Destiny Takes More Than You

When you feel stuck you feel alone. You've tried everything. You've found the right people. You've gone to the right schools and moved in to the right neighborhood. You're driving the right car and wearing the right clothes. You've joined the right organizations. And you still feel stuck.

Some things you cannot do in your own strength. You are not in pursuit of Destiny alone. You don't have to figure it out all by yourself. God has appointed people and reserved resources for your future. Getting to Destiny is about more than planning and also more than a series of accidental or serendipitous events.

Destiny is both a promise and a process. God will show you the promise, and the process must unfold to prepare and position you. That process must include a strategy to break through obstacles that stand between you and what you desire. Calm down your spirit; God will give you a strategy for Destiny.

That last sentence can be difficult to accept in our make-it-happen culture. You think it's up to you. You think all you need is preparation, perseverance, and purpose. You've got all of that and you're ready to take off—you're in touch with your Warrior Spirit. You're a beast at making it happen. You don't need assertiveness training. You'll stand up for your rights. You're ready to fight for your destiny. You'll ask for that promotion or raise, or introduce yourself to the head of the company you want to work for. Every day, you wake up charged and ready. You're strong enough to meet anything that dares stand in your way. But you're stuck. What good is all that strength if you don't have God's direction to use it?

Strength in the wrong place is weakness. That's true of anyone's gift. If you're not using your greatest asset in the right way, it's a weakness. Your greatest strength might be your undoing because it is turned to weakness if you're fighting the wrong issue or the wrong person, or for the wrong reason. You may be fighting the very person who can help you get to Destiny. You may be fighting the family that is your support system as you work tirelessly to arrive at Destiny. You may be fighting the one friend who is strong and loving enough to tell you the truth about yourself. You may be fighting a situation because it doesn't look like an opportunity.

A fighting spirit twenty-four seven may be hindering your pursuit of Destiny. Don't completely annihilate your Warrior Spirit, be battle-ready. But strive to be in control of it; use your warrior skill set effectively and only when necessary. If you're a make-it-happen person, you may be trying to do it all, doing battle every day to make your dreams come true. Your hindrance? Trying to build your dream without the Dreammaker. Getting to Destiny involves so much more than what you can do. Know this: When God works in the midst of your goals you will reach them. You definitely have a role to play, but so does God.

Distinguishing God's responsibility from your own is hard. That divine-human partnership is tough to figure out. Find that balance of doing all you can and trusting God to work out the rest.

A farmer was standing alongside his field, looking at his abundant harvest—beautiful, even rows of all types of vegetables. A neighbor drove by and commented, "Just look at what God has done!" The farmer replied, "Yes, but surely you remember what it looked like when God had it all alone!"

Destiny becomes reality when you partner with God. It's a balance of secular and sacred, the delicate balance of faith and action. At times you will move forward in the firm faith of your appointment with Destiny. Other times you will operate in your skill set, simply doing the things you're best at doing.

The difficulty with this collaborative effort is that you don't get to call all the shots, nor can you lock God into a formula. God may use the least likely source for your destiny. God can speak through enemies, children, or the infomercial you're watching at three o'clock in the morning when you can't sleep. Be open to listening to God. Let God fight the battles you can't win by yourself.

Do not attack every situation like a warrior. Sometimes you do not need to win a fight, you need a God-given strategy. You need a strategy because fighting doesn't prevent your issues from getting in your way, won't keep you from imagining insults and enemies where none exist, and can't stop you from overreacting. A godly strategy won't let your boss's thoughtless remark cause you to quit the job that will lead you to Destiny.

You need a godly strategy to handle the internal defaults that have gotten you stuck because Destiny requires you to live beyond the temporary, inconvenient challenges. A strategy will restrain you so you won't spend the money you're saving for school on a new car, and when you have a strategy, you can be happy driving the old car with tidy savings in the bank. Strategy will prevent you from making permanent decisions based on temporary situations and thwarting Destiny.

You are God's investment and the Almighty has a great interest in your success. God has a purpose in you achieving your dream; you help fulfill the divine plan for humanity. God is using you; you are not using God. That is one certain way that you can know God will give you a winning strategy—when your destiny is part of a larger good.

Don't misunderstand me. At times you will have to fight *for* Destiny, but you can't possibly fight your way *to* Destiny. Destiny always requires more than your skill set.

If you're stressed and strained fighting a battle from which you can't retreat and you feel you can't win, recognize God is in the midst of that battle. God is with you. See more in the battle than just a fight. See the Almighty.

God is a strategist who will take the storm you're in and blow you into a new arena. And God's strategy won't just take you to a new opportunity; it will keep you there. Divine strategy is for the long haul, to keep you in the fullness of Destiny. Resources without strategy lead to poverty. People without a strategy soon lose resources. All the external components for success, without strategy, will not last. Lack of strategy is why lottery winners can get millions and be broke two or three years later. Pray for resources all you like, but I would rather pray for a godly strategy. When God gives you a strategy, you can overcome anything.

But God can't give you a strategy if you think the battle is yours. When you think the battle is yours, you're giving God a strategy. When you humble yourself and admit, "I don't know,"

God will give you a strategy for every situation you confront. You may not understand God's strategy, but follow it. It may seem stupid, pointless, or even downright unreasonable, but follow it.

I admire people who have a Warrior Spirit, even when they become their own worst enemy because they can't recognize it's time to stop fighting and be still with God. I like them because they're always at the ready. The polar opposite to the Warrior Spirit—the Wimpy Spirit—makes me crazy. That person does nothing but sit still and procrastinate waiting for God. They say, "Well, I'll just pray about it." They use waiting on God as an excuse for their own lack of engagement. "If God means for me to have it, I'll have it," they mutter.

Destiny will not appear on your doorstep and introduce herself. While there is a spiritual dynamic to Destiny, it is not solely spiritual. *You* have to be engaged in the process. God definitely plays a role, but so must you. Again, that divine-human partnership is tough to figure out. But as the saying goes, work as if Destiny depends totally on you and pray as if it all depends on God.

Destiny Requires More Than Luck, Anointing, or Natural Talent

I've heard many share their journey and lament that they tried and tried and did everything they could until they could do nothing more. They sigh and say, "And then, I hit a stroke of luck...," talking about the kind of break you can't explain with logic or reason, the opportunity that comes without invitation or explanation. The chance meeting in the elevator or standing in line at Starbucks. Maybe it was something that inspired them to come up with an idea, solution, or invention. That pivotal moment brought hard work, talent, and skill to a divinely orchestrated opportunity that ushered in Destiny. It was a serendipitous moment that changed their life. They can't explain it and don't understand it, but they know that breakthrough was completely out of their power and ability.

When that happens, you are left with gratitude.

There's a lot of talk in some church circles about being anointed. It's a way of acknowledging a person's destiny. But too often I've seen this concept distorted into an exemption from hard work and sacrifice. God can position you in places where the odds say you would never be, but the positioning comes after preparation. None of us is exempt from getting training, acquiring knowledge, paying dues, or gaining experience. You still need preparation, no matter how much anointing you have.

The same principle applies to natural talent. Preparation—formal or informal—is a prerequisite for Destiny. Some people get what they need from attending great institutions of higher learning. But other people gain their preparation in the school of life—those are the ups and downs that toughen us, strengthen us, and give us wisdom for what lies ahead.

No matter how talented you are, no matter how lucky or strong your anointing, you must be willing to do what is necessary to reach your destiny. The actions required of you may be difficult, they may be uncomfortable, and they will be challenging, but your God-directed strategy will get you there. Preparation may take longer than you'd hope or planned, but keep going until you are face-to-face with success. There really is no such thing as an overnight success. All the people we consider successful—whether on television or in movies or in the community, even in the pulpit—have paid dues to get there.

An accomplished pianist gave a concert, and at a reception following his performance, a woman said, "I would give anything to be able to play the piano like you do." The man replied, "No you wouldn't." The woman looked puzzled. The pianist explained, "You wouldn't practice for fifteen hours a day, seven days a week. You wouldn't practice until your hands become stiff and sore. You wouldn't give up having a social life because you're on the road performing more often than not." The woman considered the man's comments and realized she was not willing to make such an investment.

She was unwilling because being a concert pianist wasn't her destiny.

Just because you're gifted to do a task doesn't mean you won't have to work at it to live your destiny. That you're willing to work at it is a sign that you are pursuing your calling. Most people only pursue what they love. It's the only thing that can make a person work at something for hours without getting paid. Preparation is hard work. It's not glamorous and it's tiresome. Don't let lack of preparation hinder you. Remember the wise saying: "If you fail to plan, you plan to fail.

CHAPTER 11

Learn from the Destiny of Others

Step into Greater Exposure

God is a great strategist who will call and then lead you to Destiny, but it's critical to have at least one human being who can guide you in the quest. Listening to a wise mentor and learning from the experiences of others in pursuit of Destiny can boost you past mistakes you may make while trying to do everything on your own. You need someone in your life who has successfully navigated the territory you're trying to cross.

If you're a husband who's experiencing marital tension because working and taking college classes keeps you from helping with the kids at home, talk with a successful man who overcame that same challenge. Talk to a successful business owner who had to file bankruptcy after the first business failure or someone who became a success despite flunking out of college, despite a prison record, or despite having no support at home to keep going. No one has a perfect journey to Destiny, and talking with a mentor who has experienced similar trials can help you realize there's nothing wrong with you. Everyone has setbacks, makes dumb decisions, and hits some hard bumps while trying to succeed. What you're going through is the dues you pay to take the ride.

Once you align with God and agree to take the ride, God begins putting things in motion. When the student is ready for guidance, the teacher will appear. When you are positioned toward Destiny, the mentor you need will appear. But you must be looking and you must be open to instruction, guidance, and wise counsel. When you say yes to Destiny, introductions will be made that you can't explain and you will develop associations that money could not buy.

Sound exciting? Let it happen. The best mentoring relationships evolve naturally. It is a relationship that calls for both parties to be willing participants. There are plenty of successful people willing and eager to share their knowledge with someone else. Look for opportunities that are beneficial to your pursuit of Destiny.

You want a successful mentor, of course. Otherwise, why bother? The best choice of a mentor should be someone who is successful at living a full life. A person who is effective in business but whose personal life is in shambles is not living in Destiny. A person whose financial gain is acquired by cheating or mistreating others is not living in Destiny. That's not the person you want to take advice from, except how not to do something!

A good mentor will encourage you to have patience in the process because that person already knows that Destiny takes time. A mentor knows the pitfalls of the journey. A good advisor knows how to get back up after a tumble and can help you in the sometimes painful process of standing after life knocks you down. The wisdom of a successful person you admire can build your confidence and encourage you to try new things and take calculated risks. An effective mentor also will be honest with you and advise you when you're not ready for the next step as well as challenge you to stop being afraid to take the next step and move forward.

Mentors help you learn the ropes, put you in apprenticeship programs, and lend insight into the direction that will maximize your time and opportunities. They help humble you in a positive way because they remind you that you still have more to learn. Mentors guide you to new prospects and encourage you to take risks. They let you know you have more growing to do and keep you humble. A seasoned advisor can help you navigate the strategy of your life.

Heeding the sage advice of an accomplished professional helps pave for you a smoother, less circuitous route than he or she had to tread. Mentorship decreases your learning curve. When the words of a good teacher are heeded, you lessen the possibility of mistakes, which can save you time, money, and relationships. A strong bond with a trusted advisor can help you gain ground in your chosen field much more quickly.

Are You One of the Bootstrap People?

Mentors can't help some people. You've heard the stories of people who claimed, "No one helped me. I made it all on my own." The bootstrap people who have made great strides often are not good candidates for mentorship because they are by nature independent. But even those who seek to make it on their own will eventually experience decreased momentum along the journey because they will have exhausted their internal resources. They may hit a wall after success is achieved and need a mentor to help them know how to handle power or wealth or fame or raising their children to have a motivation to find their own destiny.

People who pride themselves on doing it all alone have usually paid a great price for being loners. They might have saved themselves years of struggle or mistakes simply by being willing to listen to someone who has already been there. And there's always somebody who's been there! Rather than re-create the wheel, find a mentor who's been there and done that!

Reading and research are important tools to equip you with knowledge, but mentoring has the added benefit of stocking your decisions with wisdom that someone else has paid for. Imagine the mistakes a plumber would make without apprenticeship! Who would want a physician who had never been an intern? Would you want a surgeon who had never participated in the procedure alongside someone with greater experience? I was in a restaurant one day and two waiters walked up to the table. Since ours was a party of just two, it seemed odd to have two waiters. The lead waiter said, "Good morning! My name is Will and my associate behind me is Helen." Helen was in training, so she mostly observed and learned. Books can tell you what to do but mentoring will show you how to do it! There's nothing like having a hands-on experience.

I love to use a four-step approach to a teacher-learner relationship. First, watch me do it. Second, do it with me. Third, I'll do it with you. Fourth, I'll watch you do it. An advisory relationship using this approach can build your confidence. You work better when you have certainty about your level of knowledge, and being validated by mentorship creates confidence and raises the comfort level for all involved.

Years ago, we watched Harpo Studios bring new star power to television as Oprah Winfrey mentored Dr. Phil into his own television brand. Later, we watched Dr. Phil mentor The Doctors. In the television world, these are called spin-offs, because one entity or personality spins off an already popular show to create a new show or brand. In corporate America the term sometimes used is *sponsors*. These are the people who help you break through corporate barriers to reach new heights that would be impossible without someone who introduced you to the next level and the next level to you. In the business world, there are financiers, known as venture capitalists, who look for small companies with great potential for growth to invest in them. Peter Fenton is a forty-something venture capitalist who saw the future of Twitter and invested when the company had only twenty-five employees. Today, Twitter has more than five hundred million users who send out hundreds of millions of tweets each day.

Mentors don't create your talent, but they certainly enhance what you have to offer. Even the Bible shows case after case of mentoring. The great apostle Paul mentored Timothy, a young pastor in the early Christian church. In Matthew 4:19, Jesus mentored his disciples simply by saying, "Follow me and I'll make you fishers of men." Imagine how lost the early church would have been if it had leaders who had not mentored new generations of leadership.

Mentoring Begins Where Education Ends

> "Older siblings get more total-immersion mentoring with their parents before younger siblings come along. As a result, they get an IQ and linguistic advantage because they are the exclusive focus of their parents' attention."
>
> Jeffrey Kluger

In its purest form, parenting is about nature providing mentoring for the young. It's an admission that behaviors that seem instinctual may not come without modeling. Whether a bear is training its young to fish, a lioness is teaching her young to hunt, or a father is training his son to work, mentoring prepares a mentee for a successful experience in a fresh environment. In our purest understanding of society we are never truly independent of each other, but are instead interdependent.

As significant as education may be to professional success, education without mentoring doesn't ensure true success. Many years ago, the term *on-the-job training* was used as secular companies began to realize that the experience of the prepared must exceed the education of the novice. A résumé may profess the necessary qualifications for an applicant to apply for a position, but if that position is to be maintained, acclimatization to the organization's culture and the environment requires mentoring. In its purest expression, the term *sponsor* means one who pays for the project or activity carried out by another.

Recently, we made some staffing shifts in one of my organizations and were able to hire highly qualified people with contemporary skill sets required by ever-changing technology. Fast-forward twelve months, and I noticed that while many aspects of the job had become much more innovative, there was still a lag in productivity. Under the time crunch of our fast-paced organization, some of the newer people began to decline in progress largely because they knew how to perform the task but had not perceived the unspoken rules that exist in any infrastructure. I realized after a steady decline in productivity, along with costly mistakes and a sluggish work atmosphere, that mentoring was needed to help these most astute employees perform optimally. I brought back some of my older team members as consultants to train the new ones. The new people had the benefit of technology but lacked sensitivity to tried-and-true practices. I called the former employees to teach the new ones, even though the recent hires had great skills, because the newbies lacked the rhythm and protocol of the organization.

The final challenge was to get the old regime to provide mentoring without promoting antiquated ideologies or sabotaging the new creativity through intimidation. I learned that the philosophical understanding of the company was as important as embracing contemporary technology and business savvy.

Some knowledge is taught and some is caught. Many preachers go to Bible colleges and seminaries and gain great knowledge, but nothing they read in a book can prepare them to console a couple whose child is dying of cancer. They need an advisor to help them provide comfort to the family without falling apart themselves. Business majors can learn all the mechanics of building a company in the classroom. But mentorship teaches the voice inflection, the smile, the tilt of the head, and the exchange of pleasantries needed to connect with potential investors. An experienced counselor will help you keep your head up after you've been turned down for the twelfth time. The classroom offers a wealth of knowledge, but a mentor guides you in gaining the finer qualities needed to cultivate success. Mentors can answer the what-ifs that have never been written in a book.

Do You Need a Mentor?

How do you know whether you need a mentor? When all that is within you hasn't produced the expected outcomes, you need to enhance *what* you know with *whom* you know. There's someone who's been where you are and can help you step forward. God often answers prayer *with* people rather than *for* them. Many times the solutions you seek are provided by the people with whom you have relationships. Such connections will be your greatest resource, so protect them at all cost. These associations are more than simply mentors to mentees. They often are the critical conduits that empower you to be in the right frame of mind and the right setting to evolve to your next level. You can't reach new vistas without expanding your circle with new affiliations. The newness can be scary yet at the same time exhilarating! A life that lacks spontaneity and adventure has become predictable. If your life can be defined as a droll existence void of Destiny, then it's time to take a step!

Destiny requires a commitment to lifelong learning. No matter how much you think you know, always be willing to take another step of growth to your destiny. Failing to grow into new horizons can blind you to the beauty of life's adventures. You become like a plant that's outgrown its container. Have you ever purchased or been given a plant that grew to the confines of its container? If you decide to shift the plant to a larger pot, you may notice that the roots have grown to the shape of the receptacle that holds it. If you hadn't replanted it into something larger, the plant would remain the same size. That happens to people, too. They grow only to the confines of their environment and will grow no further without being taken to a new arena. If you're the brightest in your circle of associates, you need a new circle, a wider circle. If you're the most accomplished, broaden your group. You will be able to stretch yourself so much further once you determine not to let your current situation define or constrain you.

Add someone to your life who is smarter, more knowledgeable or accomplished than you and make learning from that person's experience part of your destiny. A mentor will push you to grow and help you move into a larger arena to gain new exposure and expand your knowledge. With the right mentor, you will evolve into new circles, and as you do there are some ground rules to consider.

First, forget about status or recognition when you move into your new circle. You may be lauded in the circle you came from, but you may have to serve in this one. In short, humility is the key to entering new levels.

The question I am most often asked by people when the topic of mentoring comes up is, "How do I gain access to people who are doing what I would love to do?" Our late president John F. Kennedy defined it best in the statement "Ask not what your country can do for you, ask what you can do for your country." In principle, Kennedy was saying what all mentees must understand. Your needs aren't as attractive to busy people as their own. What you can get from them is not their primary concern, so the relationship should be focused on seeking opportunities to add value to those you want to glean information from. In the process of giving what you have, you will gain what you do not. It is better to be a doorkeeper to your future than to be a prince of your past!

Second, the biblical principle of "ask, seek, and knock" is prudent advice for gaining a higher level of access. Most people really enjoy talking about themselves and the things that concern them. Their personal journey is often what they are most passionate about. Employ this threefold philosophy and begin a dialog with a potential mentor by saying, "I am amazed at how you do this!" As opposed to, "I don't know how to do this." The mentor's point of interest is often not as effective when it begins with you.

In a sponsorship class designed to coach those seeking funding from corporations, one of my great takeaways was that the days of coming to a company and simply asking for what you need without first understanding what they need are over. Today's businesses are not as interested in budgeting large sums of money for charitable causes solely as write-offs as they were once were. They are interested in forming partnerships that enhance their corporate mission, values, and concerns. Before asking them for money, do your homework to effectively understand what the company needs and how what you do intersects with their interests, making it worthwhile for them to engage with you.

In a similar fashion, most successful people do not give to what doesn't reward them. If you work for your mentor, the reward for the employer is increased productivity and expertise. Your employer will invest in you to expand the company's talent base. Some corporations will establish intern or training programs for students to ensure a cadre of talent is available for the industry. Companies will pay to have you trained for next-level opportunities, but often with the caveat that you must work for them a certain number of years. They view these instruction opportunities as an investment in you with an anticipated return. If you do not work for a prospective mentor, you would be wise to determine how you can add value to them. Use your creativity to move beyond the nickel-and-dime stage of time investment into the rich experience of priceless hours of focused attention! When you have the opportunity to engage a mentor, don't waste the valuable time you've been given with him or her.

It's like buying a watch. You don't purchase a quality timepiece simply because it matches your clothing. You don't make the purchase for aesthetic purposes alone; it's more important to have the correct time. Similarly, not having the right sense of time to engage your mentor will quickly move you from asset to liability, even gross pain in the derriere! Instead, carefully choosing a few questions to ask at the right time can be the gateway to gaining rich information.

The art of communication is much like music: timing is everything. Sometimes the composition calls for fortissimo and at other times pianissimo. The silence between the notes is just as important as the notes themselves. When seeking time with a mentor, sometimes you may need to come on strong, but know how to take a softer approach also. When you need to engage a mentor, maybe the smart thing to say is, "Fred, please allow me to take you to lunch," as opposed to "Fred, when can I get on your calendar and share my struggles with you?" You can't have a positive outcome if your teacher is secretly wishing you would go play in traffic! Don't be a nuisance!

Knocking before entering is a common courtesy in an office or a home. It is also true with getting attention from those whose wisdom and insight you seek. People who are presumptuous and enter parameters where they haven't been granted access are quickly escorted out and the opportunity is lost. It is better to knock on the door and wait to enter than to push your way in and risk getting escorted out! New relationships require care and time. They cannot withstand the same liberties as old associations. When you establish a relationship with a mentor, give it time to grow to a point of familiarity. No matter what the nature of the mentorship, seeking permission is always a sign of respect.

Third, know the value of on-the-job training. Admittedly, education can do much to prepare you for job performance. But it does little to equip you for the environment in which the job must be performed. NASA trains its astronauts for what is called EVA. Extravehicular activity simulates the conditions where a proposed astronaut will have to function in the weightless atmosphere of space. This training is done in a controlled environment that enables the astronaut to experience a simulated equivalent of what it will feel like to function in a nongravitational environment. While few of us will work in outer space, many of us are ultimately required to work in situations and environments that are not the controlled environment where we learned our craft. Really strong mentoring enables the mentee to adjust to the circumstances surrounding the project where he or she is to perform.

Several years before he became a household name, Tyler Perry held auditions with my wife and me for actors for our new play, *Woman Thou Art Loosed*. We were instructed by Mr. Perry to give them no indication of approval while the actors auditioned. No matter how well the audition went, we were to be expressionless throughout. Boy, was that hard! Some of them were excellent vocalists. He later explained that part of the process was to discover how well the aspiring actor could maintain focus, even if the crowd was not responsive.

Anyone who cooks can prepare food in his or her own kitchen. They work in a controlled environment that is self-designed. Home cooking can be done at your own pace and is set up for your style. But cooking professionally is a game changer. This reminds me of a popular television show, *Hell's Kitchen*. The show teaches professional chefs what it takes to compete on a higher level. If you've ever seen it, you will immediately understand how different one level is from the other. It becomes quickly clear why the show is called what it is!

Take the Tour

Most visitors want a tour guide when traveling in a foreign country. Tourists often secure the services of someone who is familiar with the territory beyond the sightseeing attractions. This is particularly true when a visitor doesn't want to spend precious vacation days guessing what sights are available and stumbling along paths of confusion and perhaps even danger. They want to go directly to the historical places or the important spots of interest so that the trip is maximized. No one would want to fly all the way to Egypt, get off the plane, and look around wondering, "Which way are the pyramids?" So why would you or I get the wonderful opportunity to gain access to Destiny's next level only to stare aimlessly, wondering, "Which way do I go?"

A good mentor is like a tour guide who shows you the sights you've maybe heard about but have never seen before. You can take yourself to the common, well-traveled places. You want someone to take you where most others never get to go. I like to say that *mentor* should be spelled *m-e-n-t-o-u-r*, because it is an unbelievable blessing to have someone open doors and tour you around what's next. I was in Kiev, the capital city of the Ukraine, a few years ago. It was so exciting to be in a part of the world where I had never been. A group of us secured a tour guide who enhanced our travel experience by showing us far more than most tourists get to see. Real tour guides take you beyond the tourist sites that are designed to impress you and look good. The best ones lead you through an immersive experience into the culture and cuisine of the locals. Finding the right guide gives you an opportunity to partake of the organic experience and not the synthetic experience that most foreigners mistake for the culture of the country!

Your mentor should know the lay of the land you are seeking. For example, it would be hard for someone who's never raised a child to give parenting advice. A person who has never held a job cannot tell you how to make your way up the corporate ranks. When you want sound advice on financial investments, you probably don't want to consult someone who has always survived on public assistance.

Finally, recognize that someone to whom you will not be accountable cannot mentor you. Imagine the impossibility of a mentor relationship with someone whom you will not share the full realities of your struggles and success. That would be a frustrating experience for both the mentor and the mentee. Accountability requires transparency; therefore, you have to establish a level of trust with your mentor that will allow you the vulnerability of exposing your deficiencies and insecurities. Most people wear their accomplishments as a camouflage to hide their inadequacies. Mentors get to look behind the façade to help you fill in the blanks that are masked from public view. They need to know how the job is affecting you emotionally. They need access to information about the areas at home that are in crisis because of your accomplishments. If you keep up a wall with your mentor, he or she will never be able to penetrate your mind to address the real challenges you face. You will probably gain a few helpful tips, but you won't reap the full benefit of someone walking alongside you on your Destiny journey.

Most of us can excel in one or two areas of life with little assistance. Mentors will help you develop a 360-degree range of success. That doesn't mean every area of your life will run smoothly at all times. Most of us are dealing with some level of trouble or challenge at any point in our lives. We all need someone we trust to serve as a check and balance to help us live the full live we desire. Mentors ask you the hard questions. When you're soaring high from career advancement, your mentor will inquire about the other plates you're juggling. It's wonderful to have a great career, but if your marriage is falling apart because of it, the success may come at a higher price than you want to pay. You've got lots of money in the bank now, but your mentor will ask how you're inspiring your kids to have their own goals and dreams apart from your accomplishments.

Not all mentoring is the same. Some is designed to help you maximize where you are. This kind comes when one hasn't exhausted the potential of current opportunity. To be sure, mentoring cannot claim to vest the recipient with the opportunity or the skill set necessary to reach Destiny. But it can help you better utilize what you possess to reach your fullest potential. Though this type of mentoring doesn't create new opportunities, it does give you a different look at how to better manage where you are. Much like a stylist who comes in your closet and shows you original ways to present your wardrobe. People who are gifted can draw new opportunities out of old apparel. The clothes aren't new but they can appear so when they are presented correctly. Or people who help families in crisis mentor them with novel ways to navigate the family through past perils. In most instances, the opportunities may not be new but the perspective must be fresh or the mentoring is a gross waste of time.

Mentoring at its best affords you the insights that affirm the skills and acumen you need to evolve into next-level thinking.

But if you have exhausted your opportunities and feel anxious to graduate into the life you deserve, mentoring often gives you the tour guide view of how to revolutionize your thinking as you evolve in your experiences. What's really wonderful is that most people who seek mentoring are ready to be exposed to new sociological constructs and are anxious to shift their efforts from where they've been before to where they want to go.

There is a vast difference between teaching a person to understand with skills and facts verses mentoring, which helps them adapt to the entire process of when to use what and how. Many people leave college thinking, "I have a degree and I'm ready." Yes, the degree has given you the tools, but mentoring shows you how to best use those tools and prepares you to work what you know in the environment where you must perform. In years past we had apprenticeships. They were basically mentoring as OJT, on-the-job training. It prepared a mechanic, a plumber, or an accountant to adapt to the unexpected circumstances of construction. Yes, you may know how to solder the pipe, but you didn't expect it to be right beside an electrical line! Mentoring helps you achieve in new environments an expected end. A good mentor will let you explore the territory from a holistic perspective, unlike teaching laboratories, which are controlled environments.

An ounce of prevention is worth a pound of cure, my mother would say! You can head off many issues if you are accountable to someone. Everyone needs a trusted advisor to serve as a guide on the path to Destiny. A few creatures in the animal kingdom have the gift of 360-degree sight, but human beings are not among those species. You can't be aware of your frontal, rear, and peripheral vision simultaneously. We all need someone who has our back who can be our backup eyes and ears in the places we may miss. A Destiny-oriented person is always looking ahead, focusing on the next leg of the journey. Be sure you have others you trust helping you look out for your sides and your back. Just like many newer model vehicles have warning lights in the side-view mirrors to let you know a car is in your peripheral view, your mentor cautions you to be mindful of what you cannot see. Take your mentor into the places in your life where you are under attack. You can figure out a safe passage together that you couldn't do alone! From finances to family, mentors help you balance the budget of life!

Choose Your Mentors à la Carte

If your life is as complex as mine, you may realize that mentors don't always come as one-stop shopping. It is possible to have different people from whom you receive mentoring. You can have one person who mentors you financially while another mentors you spiritually. The most happily married couple you know may be living on minimum wage salaries while your investment banker may be on the brink of divorce. Talk to the happy couple about marriage and talk to the investment banker about money. We are multifaceted human beings. We are emotional, spiritual, sensual, relational, physiological, intellectual beings. While many mentors can span a wide range of needs, not all are suited to bring value to every area of your life. The person who excels at business may be a great professional resource, but may not be the best person to give you guidance on weight loss and healthy eating. Your mentor may not appear to be the person for you, but remain open to whom God sends.

You may be seeking a mentor who affirms everything you do, but God may send you someone who is more critical of your actions and decisions. If you're middle-aged, your mentor may be someone younger. Don't close your mind to the possibilities of who can offer you guidance. You may need a younger mentor to help your business opportunities grow through social media. Perhaps the thirty-something self-made millionaire can coach you in developing your retirement portfolio for a more comfortable life when you stop working.

Mentoring may be the booster shot you need if you feel your life is lagging in certain critical areas. A strong relationship will cause you to redeem the time you may have lost trying to find your own way. A mentor can make the difference between success and failure. In church we refer to this relationship dynamic as discipleship. The root word of *discipleship* is where we get its related word *discipline*. Without it, most people never achieve their goals because Destiny requires one to have the capacity for control. As you develop the ability to regulate yourself, you will wisely use time. Order always increases productivity. Yes, it is difficult to discipline yourself, hence the accountability of mentors!

As you take the steps necessary to enhance your ever-so-brief stay on this planet, you will want to develop self-mastery. Shed the indifference of failure for the drive of achievers. You will learn how early to rise, with whom and where to invest time, what to ignore, and what to engage. This is a fabulous time in your life to catch up and overtake what God has in store for you!

Middle-aged and older persons can begin to feel life holds no further opportunities: "If it hasn't happened by now, it won't happen." You don't have the luxury of indulging in such limited thinking. Never forget that Harland Sanders was sixty-five years old when he sought to franchise his now-famous chicken recipe as Kentucky Fried Chicken. Actor Morgan Freeman has been acting on stage, on television, and in films for most of his life, but he did not achieve renown as an actor until he was in his fifties when he earned critical acclaim for his roles in *Driving Miss Daisy* and *Glory*. Destiny has her own timetable, and just because you haven't gotten there yet doesn't mean that you won't.

A younger mentor may energize and remind you of what you still have to offer. An older mentor can serve as living proof that what you desire can happen for you, too. Yes, there is someone willing to mentor you no matter what your age.

Destiny is a journey made of a series of stops, rather than a single destination. As you engage in your life's calling, you will evolve, grow, and make turns and shifts. Your Destiny journey includes legacy. God calls you to a task to make life better, and the work you do should have an impact long after you have stepped away. So make your connection with a fellow traveler who is successfully maneuvering the heavy, fast-moving traffic and allow them to guide you to places you have never been and reveal sights you have never seen. Life is exciting, so enjoy the journey. You aren't on the road alone. Whether you are moving too fast and feel like you're about to crash, chugging along slowly while everyone zooms by, or parked in the rest station because you're out of gas, there's someone willing to help you. Let God use your mentor to help guide you to Destiny.

CHAPTER 12

Failure Is Not the End of Destiny

Step in Your Mess and See the Value of Your Mistakes

Because we live in such a results-dominated society, it is tempting to see failure as an experience to be avoided at any cost. We all want to give the appearance of success, even if we are failing miserably. We rack up huge credit card debts to make it appear we are more successful than we actually are. A wife may rave publicly about a husband who barely speaks to her at home. An employee may fabricate certain aspects of his job responsibilities so others will think he's the top dog at work. Others pretend to know wealthy or influential persons so they can appear socially or politically well connected. Parents may embellish their children's accomplishments so they do not seem mediocre.

The dread of failure leads to a "safe success" philosophy to ensure that no mistakes will be made. No risks are taken. Destiny eludes those who live this way. That's ironic considering our regrets in life don't come from failing; they come from not trying—failing to try.

Destiny seekers must be willing to take some faith risks. Some of those risks will never pay off, but others will succeed. And a few will succeed beyond your wildest imagination. Destiny seekers possess what has been labeled "the indomitable human spirit." A contemporary phrase that expresses this sentiment is, "You can't keep a good man (or woman) down." Going where Destiny calls means trying again after failure.

Get Up Again . . . and Again

W. Mitchell was burned beyond recognition in a terrible motorcycle accident. Four years later, he was paralyzed from the waist down in an airplane crash. The combination of the two tragedies would cause most people to give up on life, but not Mitchell. He ran for Congress under the slogan "Not just another pretty face." He also became a millionaire, a respected public speaker, a happily married husband, and a successful businessperson.

Failure does not have to be the end of your dance with Destiny. It can become what gets you back out on the floor again. You still have something to accomplish. The Supremes, one of the greatest R & B groups of the Motown era, for years were known as the "No Hit Supremes." But they kept on singing. Billy Graham's first love refused to marry him because she didn't think he'd amount to much. But he married Ruth Bell and not only became one of the great evangelists of his time, but established a ministry legacy that his children continue. Many great Bible characters experienced failures, but God continued to seek them out for a purpose. The upside of failure is knowing "as bad as I've messed up, God still wants me for something.

My Creator is looking for me, reaching out to me, guiding me to reach my destiny."

An executive caused a loss of $10 million at the company for which he worked. The CEO, when asked if he would fire the lower-level exec, responded, "No, I've got too much invested in him to ever get rid of him!" God has invested a great deal in you. Even your failures are an investment that will reap benefits and dividends. Through the mishaps of life, you become stronger, better, and wiser for the journey.

Thomas Edison, nineteenth-century inventor with more than one thousand patents to his credit, was a poor student in school. His schoolmaster once referred to him as "addled," which prompted Edison's furious mother to begin homeschooling her son. Edison was a young failure. He seemed to lack the aptitude for learning when, more than likely, the boy's interest far exceeded what was being taught in the classroom. Although Edison was a failure in school, as his mother homeschooled him, she stretched his mind beyond what he ever could have conceived in a classroom. His inventions of the phonograph and the incandescent light bulb are just a few of the results of this childhood failure.

Failing can cause you to question God. Its pain and disappointment may make you doubt your purpose. You may wonder if your destiny is to be in an environment where you are not appreciated. Making sense of failure is part of the march to Destiny.

Get off the merry-go-round of perfectionism and realize failure is not a bad thing. Failure is a growing thing. If failure were all bad, many successful people would have given up long before they reached success. Many who are now highly successful entrepreneurs failed in business repeatedly, or were even bankrupt several times before achieving financial success.

Yet we don't see the failure as beneficial. Just the thought of failure makes us want to run and hide. We don't even need to actually fail to experience feelings of dread, anxiety, fear, or depression associated with failure. We hate the mere thought of failure, and one of the reasons we hate failure so much is that we associate a failed *deed* with a failed *self.*

But it's the business that failed, not you. It's the marriage that failed, not you. It's the presentation that failed to get potential investors, not you. Failure is a part of the process of reaching Destiny. It is not a personal attribute, a character flaw. Just as successful people are not perfect—no one is—people who are not successful at an endeavor are not failures. Your identity, your self-worth, your public persona are tied to your God-given destiny, not any one particular doing, whether that doing succeeds—or fails. No baseball player—not even Babe Ruth, Hank Aaron, or Barry Bonds—hits a home run every time he comes up to bat. Many times they strike out. Those few occasions when they hit a flyer out of the ballpark add up to their stellar stats and make the trip up to bat worth it time and time again.

We never see the value of our failures in the abyss of our downward spiral. Only when the smoke has cleared are we able to assess what happened and say, "I didn't know it then, but that was the best thing that could have happened to me." Redeeming value is in our failures. In fact, what looks like failure to us may actually be part of a bigger divine strategy to bring circumstances and actions and resources into place, as well as to strengthen us for the heavy weight of future success.

Find Reward in Failure

My father died when I was a teenager, and so my mother had to teach me how to drive an automobile. She would tell me often,

"Keep your eyes on the road, baby. The car will always go in the direction of your eyes." If you keep your eyes on the road to Destiny, your life will follow. Keeping your eyes on the road when pursuing Destiny becomes tedious and boring, as is often the case after a failure. Know that you are a work in progress. Look for the signs of advancement and celebrate your moments of growth.

You cannot zap yourself to Destiny. The trek to Destiny is not a "Beam me up, Scotty" *Star Trek* experience. Celebrate accomplishments at strategic points that let you know you're on the right track. The road to Destiny is a process. That process has highs and lows. You will have some failures, but most of the time you will be confronted by the fear of failure, rather than actual failure. Learn to live with the fear. Otherwise, you will accomplish nothing because you choose safety and security.

You will have times of conflict, chaos, confusion, discomfort, challenges, doubts, and fears as you pursue Destiny. These feelings will not go away unless you learn to live with them, move forward despite them, trust God while you feel them. Waiting for your fears to subside, for conditions to be right, you will waste your life and never do what God called you to do, never pursue your destiny. The timing will never be perfect. Conditions will always be shaky. All the money you need may not be there. All the people you need may not be there. But keep going. At every turn in your Destiny path, walk with the assurance that God will bring you through trouble, through confusion, through disappointment. Either live with the threat of failure or live forever as a slave to fear. It's not what you go through that matters, it's what you *feel* about what you go through. When God calls you into Destiny, you may not know if you're doing it right or not, but keep going forward anyway. Yes, you may fail—this time, maybe even next time, or the time after that. Get up, try again. Keep going. Get over your fear of failure, because that is worse than actually failing.

Success can be frightening because of the fear of failure. If you've never really accomplished anything, you can live in failure every day and no one notices or cares. But once you have the ticket to success in hand, the thought of losing it may terrify you. The thought of public humiliation can cripple you. It's a much bigger fall from the top of Destiny's ladder than from the bottom rung. But I would rather reach great heights and risk a sharp descent than to have never experienced the fullness of life from up high.

Stop thinking something is wrong when you have problems. Stop thinking something is wrong because there's conflict. There's supposed to be conflict. Problems are part of Destiny's process. That life is supposed to be easy is a lie. That anybody can do anything *easily* is a lie. Keep moving no matter how fearful you feel as you face problems and conflict.

What does an obstetrician say when her pregnant patient complains about morning sickness and her clothes getting too tight around the waist? "That's just part of the process." Problems and conflict just go along with the process of bringing Destiny to fruition. Elements embedded on the road map to Destiny—problems, pitfalls, failures, disappointments, confusion, betrayals, and frustrations—are all signs you're on the right road.

Get over your feelings. Don't act on them. Act on what you've learned in the previous chapters—your God-given instinct, the draw of your divine Destiny, the order you've established in your life by setting priorities, sharpening your focus and ignoring distractions, getting to know yourself, and using the guidance of your mentors. Check yourself carefully. Make sure you have a solid plan, then act on your plans, not your fears. Destiny may be just on the other side of what you fear.

I don't like heights, but I needed to inspect the roof of a building the church was considering for purchase. It took me longer than anyone else in the congregation to get up there, but the driving force that kept pushing me to climb higher was the belief that God had provided the building. Don't let fear block God's destiny for you.

CHAPTER 13

Destiny Demands a Curious Mind

Get in Step with the Pursuit of Greater Knowledge

You don't have to know *everything* to achieve your destiny. A successful heart surgeon doesn't necessarily know how to carve the Thanksgiving turkey. His cutting knowledge is being used where he can give the greatest benefit to humanity. When you know what you need to know, you can benefit others rather than be ashamed of the limits of your knowledge. The pursuit of knowledge is an adventure rather than an admission of ignorance or limitation. The willingness to move into the vistas of greater knowledge is an important quality that will allow Destiny to open her doors to you.

But the pursuit of knowledge simply for the sake of knowing is not a good Destiny strategy. You can know a lot about a lot of different topics, but if you're not using knowledge to fulfill the destiny that gives your life purpose, what good is it? Who wants to be the person sitting at home watching *Jeopardy!*

and answering every question right? Use your knowledge for a purpose that serves humanity. It's one thing to have a knowing mind, but it's quite another to have an inquiring mind.

The journey to Destiny necessitates a curious mind. You need courage to admit what you do not know, to seek knowledge. Strive for an inquiring mind that is perpetually turned toward the far-reaching arms of knowledge. If you limit yourself to what you already know, you'll only do what you've always done, and you'll keep on getting what you've always had.

Some *do* want what they've always had. They feel more secure, more in control in the tiny confines of life rooted in ignorance. They are content in a haze of ignorance. They choke whatever and whoever is under their influence so they can manage it easily and feel in control. They refuse knowledge and growth, fearing they may not be able to manage or be in control. Examples are the small business owner who's threatened by the expansive ideas of a young recruit from a larger company; the stage mother whose management of her son's singing career limits his exposure to what she can understand and control, stifling his opportunities; and the pastor whose congregation is growing beyond his management skills, so he stifles the church's growth.

The refusal to learn is the pass that some people use to get through life without confronting reality. They cloak themselves in ignorance so they won't have to take action. Knowledge necessitates action. The responsibility of knowledge to take action is why a mother will pretend not to notice her children are being molested by their stepfather. She acts like she doesn't know because if she acknowledges what is happening, she knows she will have to report him to the police. Child protective services will invade their lives. He may lose his job and go to jail, and they may have to go on public assistance and live in public housing. She chooses ignorance because she cannot handle the responsibility, the burden of knowing.

Knowledge brings with it tremendous responsibility and awareness of a better way. Oprah often quotes Maya Angelou: "When you know better, you do better." Many thoughtless deeds are committed out of ignorance. But when you know better than to think one race is superior to another, you can no longer justify being a racist. When you know better than to threaten and intimidate others, you are obliged to treat others with courtesy and respect. When you know better than to spend all your money on payday and figure out how to pay the bills later, you are duty-bound to establish a budget and follow it. When you know that you can motivate your child better with encouragement than with criticism, you compliment what he is doing well and kindly suggest ways he can improve areas that need it. This know-better/do-better correlation is what makes knowledge such a powerful responsibility.

The decision to pursue knowledge always opens a larger space than we ever intended—Destiny. If you gain knowledge about investments, you also will learn about people who use their investments wisely or illegally. If you gain knowledge about teaching, you also gain knowledge about children, those who are sheltered and those who somehow get themselves to school because they live with a drug-addicted parent. Pursuing knowledge can cause you to learn far more than you ever intended. For some, it's just easier to be ignorant.

But ignorance will not lead you to Destiny. When I counsel families that are living beneath their destined purpose, I find the family members are angry or are relating to one another in a dysfunctional way because their memories are inaccurate or an incomplete picture of what actually occurred. All the family's members experienced the same events, but they processed the information differently. Most of us have a version of truth that is based on our perspective or the source that informs us. In a court trial, two or more eyewitnesses can report the same event differently. Sometimes you can't even trust your own eyes. When we hold inaccurate perceptions, we will judge wrongly. Prisons are full of the wrongly incarcerated because someone thought they saw something or someone, only to have DNA evidence later prove the false perception of what actually happened. Such judgments also often stunt our personal growth and disengage us from Destiny.

A closed mind will always manufacture life paralysis. It is difficult to accept the challenge of changing your views, but if you do otherwise you will not be able to grow. Consider that your perspective might be limited or even distorted.

Examine your personal narrative. Be willing to challenge your thoughts or positions. Reexamine previously held truths. You can't begin to grow or learn until you are willing to release your hold on old ideas, even your own.

Pursuit of Destiny is behavior that has been preceded by an internal change. People can't change their behavior if they will not forsake the story that they tell themselves: "It's somebody's fault that I am where I am. I should be ashamed. I will never forgive him for what he did to me!" This refusal to give up the story of blame, shame, or unforgiveness is often the culprit that paralyzes progress.

Open-minded people often reexamine situations to consider other possibilities or viewpoints that may have affected what happened. They are curious about new ideas and perspectives. Examining your own thinking isn't easy, but if you accept the challenge of Destiny, you must put your history on trial!

Stretch Yourself. Let Go and Learn!

I don't know are three of the most powerful words you can utter. That simple confession unlocks the doors to information and exposure. These three powerful words are also courageous, spoken most often by those who have a strong sense of self-worth. Curious minds utter "I don't know" because they want to stretch and extend themselves beyond what they currently know. They seek information beyond their limited sphere. Their confession of ignorance on a particular topic opens the way for teachers to enter and offer enlightenment, wisdom, insight, and information.

The acquisition of knowledge requires that we stretch ourselves to receive new information. If you've ever stretched any part of your body, you know it can be uncomfortable. It's a humbling experience for newcomers to the gym to bend over only to discover they cannot stretch down and touch their toes. But with consistent stretching, those tight muscles release and the forward bend with fingers on the floor becomes second nature.

It takes courage to admit you don't know something, and courage again to go after the knowledge to fill that void. Destiny seekers are secure in themselves, willing to admit they don't know something.

There's a saying that you can't learn to swim and hang on to the edge of the pool at the same time. The way you learn to swim is by getting in the water.

To expand your knowledge and exposure in life, let go of the easy and familiar, just like the swimming pool sidelines. Let go of a poverty mind-set to attain wealth, a single's mind-set in order to be married, a worker's mind-set to become a successful manager. Some maintain ignorance because knowledge will mean leaving the comfort of the familiar. A woman who had lived in public housing for more than twenty years married a man who took seriously his role as a husband and provider. After they had been married a few months, he forced her to discuss a topic she had managed to avoid: moving out of public housing and buying a home of their own. She became so angry at the suggestion that she threatened to divorce him. "He wants to move us out of here and into a house," she told a friend. "What would be so bad about that?" the friend asked. The newlywed woman replied, "I know I can make it in here. But he wants to get us out there, somewhere I don't know what might happen!" The woman wasn't interested in gaining knowledge about how to survive without the crutch of public assistance. Nor was she interested in gaining the knowledge a wife must have to trust her husband as a loving provider.

If you've been promoted, you can no longer always hang out with other workers at break time. They may accuse you of being uppity, but you've got a staff to manage. You can't change your life and hold on to the familiar. That's ignorance!

Destiny reveals herself to risk takers—those adventurous souls who are willing to stick more than a toe in the water. If you don't know how to swim it's foolish to jump in deep water. But once you decide to learn how to swim, it's time to let go of the edge of the pool. The edge where it's safe, familiar. Getting in deep water is scary, because no matter how careful you are or how skillful your instructor, there's a possibility that you could drown. Getting in the water is scary because it's cold. But getting in is the only way you will learn to swim. You can't learn hanging on the edge. Getting to the next level of your knowledge and ability works exactly the same way—except nobody ever drowned in deep knowledge.

Stretching your level of knowledge requires vulnerability. Be willing to experience the discomfort of ignorance, and sometimes even the shame. Position yourself in places where you can learn and grow. Accept feeling like a complete idiot because everyone but you seems to know exactly what to do. Put on your adventure cap and get in touch with the curious child inside you who's willing to ask a thousand questions, risk looking silly, and laugh at himself when a learning opportunity doesn't quite work out as planned.

Forget the Dumb Stuff!

I've become increasingly concerned over a societal trend that can be best described as a dumbing down of ideas. The acquisition of knowledge seems to have little value or meaning. The time, energy, and money spent on parole celebration as opposed to graduation parties is evidence of this. The "reality" genre of television has led to a dumbing down of entertainment. We expect less from television and the people who appear on it, and the craft and skill of acting and long hours of training and sacrifice by actors are devalued in the face of the new "reality" stars. We dumb down information to a 140-character tweet on Twitter or a brief Facebook post or a seconds-long YouTube video. The knowledge you need for Destiny won't come in a tweet or any social media post. You won't see it on Instagram.

Destiny's knowledge comes to those who are properly positioned to learn. The classroom. Your mentor. Your current job. Volunteer work. The skills, tools, and wisdom you will need to move ahead in life come through time and persistence.

The expression "I know just enough to be dangerous" indicates superficial knowledge. Such knowledge gives you a false sense of comfort about your ability to address a situation. Our society today seems to specialize in knowing just enough to be dangerous. We rely on snippets of information rather than a true pursuit of knowledge. We live in a fast culture and we like to get everything fast. Proprietary schools and online colleges often advertise to appeal to a person's desire to get an education fast. All knowledge doesn't come fast. Gaining real knowledge is like the recipe to your grandmother's stew. You slowly add ingredients and give them a chance to simmer and blend to enhance their collective flavor. Settling for dumbed-down information is like feeding yourself from vending machines when you could be feasting on Grandmama's stew.

True knowledge requires an in-depth absorption of information gained over time. With knowledge, it's hard for anyone to shake you. You can stand on your decisions and have less fear about moving forward toward the future. Seek knowledge for the sake of enlightenment and Destiny. It takes courage to be knowledgeable in a world that dumbs down information. You run the risk of being told: "You've forgotten where you came from." But you can't forget where you came from, because you *lived* there and it is your base of knowledge for all that you learn. If you grew up in an abusive home, you *know* that it was not pleasant. As you gain knowledge about how people relate in healthy households, what you learn is reinforced by your experience growing up.

Knowledge beyond your present parameters is the entrée to your future. Start reading journals and blogs and books that you've never read before. Go places you've never gone so that when God opens the door, you're not trying to get ready. Be ready. Maybe you don't like hockey, but it won't hurt to expose yourself to a game. Maybe you don't like ballet, or hip-hop music, but exposure to it will help you broaden your base of knowledge.

Feed Your Mind's Cravings

Destiny requires mental preparation, so absorb information and knowledge like a pregnant woman eats. You know how pregnant women get a craving for strange stuff that doesn't make sense to anyone else? When you are pregnant with Destiny, you start craving things that your best friend doesn't understand. But just because your bestie doesn't understand it doesn't mean that you're not moving in the direction God would have you to go.

Your craving for knowledge may even cause you to lose some friends. When you concentrate on Destiny knowledge and become interested in new subjects and are not content to sit around talking about somebody else's clothes or relationship, some people are going to pull away from you. Relax. Your real friends will give you room to improve yourself because they're trying to improve themselves, too. True friends are happy for you when you get more education, start volunteering in an organization that can expose you to people who can help your career, or start dating a man who takes you to restaurants you've never been to before.

Increased knowledge can grow you to the point where you tire of people who think in a box. You'll look at your best friend since kindergarten and wonder what happened to him. Nothing happened to him. Something happened to you! He is still Pookie who works long enough to earn a pack of cigarettes, a half tank of gas, and some hamburger money. Pookie calls you a slave because you're dedicated to your job at a moving company: "Man, all you talk about is that break-your-back job!" Pookie doesn't understand that you're gaining knowledge, learning all you can about the moving business because you realize you won't be young forever, and by the time you get too old to move furniture, you want to own your own moving company. What happened? Pookie is where he's always been. *You* have been growing.

The more you learn and are exposed to new things, the harder it is to stay in the same circles. As you expand in knowledge, you will look back and wonder how you were ever satisfied with a football game, the fellas, a pack of cigarettes, and a six-pack of beer to wash down your hot dogs. Knowledge pulls you away from that into a larger arena. Sure, you'll still enjoy a football party with the boys, but it's no longer what you live for. You know there's more.

Accept the fact that your craving for knowledge will be threatening to some. They won't understand why you spend time and money to go back to school or why you'll take a lesser paying apprenticeship position or why you're reading everything you can about spirituality and faith. The people who are threatened may take comfort in their ignorance, but they're like a person diagnosed with type 2 diabetes who receives a great deal of information about living with the disease—information about nutrition, exercise, stress, and how all of these factors can have an impact on blood sugar levels—who says, "Aw, I don't care what those doctors say. I'm going to eat whatever I want. I'm going to die of something anyway." And many *do* die from diabetes-related complications because they refused the knowledge that would enable them to live successfully with this chronic condition. They choose ignorance over life-enhancing knowledge. Destiny seekers choose knowledge.

Your craving for knowledge is getting you ready for God's destiny for you. Your mental preparation comes through knowledge.

Inquiring Minds Want to Know More

Are you willing to explore your mind? Are you courageous enough to venture out and learn what other people do not know? Are you willing to dust off the unused crevices in your brain to gain knowledge?

Destiny's coursework can be a bit challenging. There's no syllabus and the teachers may look unqualified. Gain knowledge from unlikely sources. Someone you eschew as insignificant may teach you Destiny's greatest lessons. Learn something from the great-aunt you think can't possibly know anything because she is old and unenlightened. Let the four-year-old who lives next door share a simple truth that enlightens you. The homeless man who perches himself on the bench outside your office every day can drop science on you if you are learning the ways of Destiny.

Knowledge comes from all types of people and sources. Open your mind to opportunities to gain knowledge and take the time to engage with those who don't look like you or think like you or act like you. They can prove to be your life's greatest teachers. Let your quest for knowledge take you places you've never gone so when God opens the door to Destiny that you've always wanted to enter, you'll be prepared.

As I said earlier, distinguishing God's responsibility from our own is hard because that divine-human partnership is tough to figure out. We all work at finding that balance of doing all we can and waiting for God to work out the rest. Seeking knowledge is what we do while we wait for God. Wait time is precious time. When we're preparing ourselves with knowledge while we wait, we're not bored or impatient or hopeless. We're learning.

While you're waiting on the career change, get all the knowledge you can about the profession. While you're waiting on the spouse, get all the knowledge you can about being a better you. While you're waiting on the financial breakthrough, get all the knowledge you can about managing money and assets so you'll be ready. Whatever you're waiting for Destiny to deliver, knowledge will take and keep you there. While you're waiting on those doors to open, be curious and use your time to get the knowledge you need to handle the new arena Destiny is beckoning you to enter.

Your mind must remain open to exposure, which comes in many forms beyond your environment, your friends, and especially your comfort zone. Condition your mind to be curious about what life has to offer. Be curious about other cultures, their family dynamics, their languages, their cuisine, and their faith. Allow your curious mind to wander into new places Destiny opens to you. Exposure opens your mind to ideas that never could have blossomed in your head. Destiny's pursuit is going to put you in unfamiliar spaces, and with each new experience, God is whetting your appetite for your next step toward Destiny, exposing you to what you will need and enjoy in your future.

CHAPTER 14

Distractions Destroy Destiny

Step Away from What Doesn't Matter

Passion takes energy. Vision takes energy. Strategy takes energy. As Destiny draws you, you will need to invest yourself there, which means you don't have time for energy-draining attitudes, feelings, and emotions—being jealous, intimidated, or scared. You have been chosen to play the role that is your destiny. You have a calling.

Are you jealous of someone who seems to have a greater talent than you? Simply do what you do. No person was meant to be someone else. Every person's destiny offers fulfillment in doing what God has destined that person to do. Be happy for that talented person and find your purpose, the calling for your unique gifts. If there's someone you envy, even if you could live their life, you wouldn't enjoy it. In fact, you'd probably be miserable because it's not *your* life.

Frustration with Destiny's process can also cause us to become envious of people who seem to have already arrived. Remember they, too, endured a process. Every success has a backstory that you cannot see.

I am not accountable for the gifts God gave someone else. God does not expect me to produce beyond the level of gifts given me. My only obligation is to use the gifts God has given me to the best of my ability.

The gifts God gave you are not the same as the gifts the Creator has given anyone else. So why look at what God has done in someone else's life and then belittle what he has done in your own life? If you compare yourself with others, you'll never be at peace. Somebody's ice will always seem colder. Someone will have more degrees, a larger bank account, a grander house, a better physique, or a greater oratorical ability. Celebrate the skin you're in and be happy pursuing your own destiny.

Know Why You Seek Destiny

Destiny is bitter when pursued just to prove something to someone—the father who left home and never sent a dime to help your mother, or the girl who rejected you in high school because you were a nerd. So if you envision Destiny as proof of something to someone, stop right here. Back up to Chapter Six (*For Destiny's Sake, Do You!*) and figure out who you want to be and why. You need a strong identity to pursue Destiny.

The secret is that it has to be bigger than you. For even if by a miracle, your self-serving dream does come to fruition, it's not going to be what you hoped if it's only for you or your ego. A desire to serve humanity, help your family, or improve yourself is stronger than your ego. Your ego motivates you to succeed because of how your success will impress others. You can't skate your way to Destiny, so you must know why you're willing to endure challenges. Making someone else envious is a poor incentive to stay faithful to Destiny's demands. Destiny is bigger than you and so must your dream be.

In a 2006 speech then-senator Barack Obama gave to a group of college students, he offered these sage words about success: "Focusing your life solely on making a buck shows a certain poverty of ambition. It asks too little of yourself. Because it's only when you hitch your wagon to something larger than yourself that you realize your true potential."

Purpose is bigger than ego and can sustain you as you travel Destiny's path. Identify your purpose and then let patience perfect you! Patience purges bad motives and clears jealous vision. It allows you to mature and increases clarity!

Destiny Starts in Your Head

Destiny is about more than simply reaching a destination. What you gain along your way to your destination is part of Destiny. You can't get to Destiny and bypass people, experiences, and lessons. Your mentors propel you to Destiny, but so do the people who do everything they can to thwart you. Successes will boost you closer to Destiny, but so will your mistakes. The lessons you learn will drive you nearer to Destiny, but so will the instruction you failed to heed. This complex mix is inextricably part of the Destiny process.

Surviving that process requires that you find joy in the details on your path to Destiny: menial jobs, demanding bosses, failed relationships, financial setbacks. Keep them in perspective. Recognize that each brings you closer to Destiny.

Remember your strategy during these long, uneventful seasons, because it gives you concrete reasons to keep pushing forward. Want your future badly enough to grab hold and not let go when the day-to-day has you feeling like a failure.

You may not *feel* like a person of Destiny when you wake up every day, but that's just your feelings. Your *head* will tell you to get up, be on time, and face the daily challenges because Destiny awaits you. Your future is not rooted in how you feel but in how you act. You cannot base your quest for Destiny on feelings. The way you feel changes based on different variables, but your mind changes based on knowledge and information. Don't give in to your feelings. Emotions are the saboteurs of Destiny. Beat your feelings into captivity through mental discipline.

Discipline says, "I may not like what I have to do today, or feel like doing it, but I know what must be done and why I have to do it." Discipline is the domain of the head. The new car you can't afford right now but feel would make you happy will wait if you have financial discipline. Discipline gets you to the gym to work out when your feelings say stay in because it's cold and rainy today. Discipline says skip the second helping; stay on the job even though your boss made you mad enough to quit; tell your child no even though she'll pout, moan, and whine for a week; stay in school even though you feel like an eternal student.

Feelings tell you to get your hair and nails done because you're a little depressed. Discipline tells you to budget in getting your hair and nails done because you need to make a good impression at your upcoming job interview.

Discipline makes decisions that take you toward Destiny. I've looked back on decisions I made and asked myself, "What was I thinking?" Our thinking can be flawed, skewed, or based on erroneous information. Right information and disciplined thinking leads to right decisions. But nobody can be spot-on in their decisions every time. Like me, you will still make some mistakes, but the likelihood of mistakes is far greater if your life is based on feelings rather than head choices. When you do make mistakes, keep a level head, reassess, and move in the direction of Destiny.

Above all else, guard what goes on in your head. Protect that space between your ears with all you've got! A soldier about to go into battle, a police officer about to make a raid, a football player headed for the playing field—they will all protect their heads with the proper gear. Protect your head so that your journey to Destiny is guided by knowledge rather than feelings. Protect your head to keep negativity out. When people doubt your abilities, when you have an attack of low self-esteem, or when you experience a setback, don't fall into a dark place from which you cannot easily emerge. Preserve your positive thoughts. Keep your thoughts in a good place. Protect the positive person inside you who is telling you that you have what it takes. Watch your self-talk. Tell yourself you will make it, no matter what happens, no matter what anyone else thinks. After Elvis Presley's very first performance, his manager told him, "You ain't goin' nowhere, son. You ought to go back to drivin' a truck." It's a good thing the King protected his head and didn't listen! His records have sold more than one billion copies.

Protecting your head is important because discouraging advice will come from the sage experts. And if you're filling your own head with negative information, you can cancel out the helpful efforts of mentors, sponsors, and advisors. If five hundred people tell you that you have what it takes, all you have to do to cancel all of that positive energy is look in the mirror and say, "No, I don't." Protect your head against others, but also against yourself.

God's opinion is the only one you need. If God says you can, that's all that matters. Listen to what God tells you. Then watch what you say to yourself. Don't tear yourself down. Don't beat yourself up. You cannot arrive at Destiny if you tell yourself that you're not good enough, not smart enough, not qualified, not attractive. Don't work against God by tearing yourself down. Reaching Destiny requires you to monitor how you talk to yourself.

Next to the voice of God, your own is the most important one you will hear. You are with you all the time, so guard how you talk to yourself. You can avoid negative people, but you can never get away from yourself. You can't escape yourself. If you're tearing yourself down, change your thoughts from negative to positive and from destructive to uplifting.

Build yourself up by speaking self-empowering words. Ward off "iffy" talk—"I wonder" or "What if"—this is nothing more than negative speculation. Guard your head against speculation about your destiny. You can't have what you are striving for in your hand until you have it in your head. Get it in your head—not in your feelings—that you can and will achieve your goals. Whatever you want, get it in your head. I vividly remember a conversation I had with my sister back in West Virginia when my wife and I had been through repeated financial challenges. I was tired of being broke. Riding in the car with my sister, I told her, "I'm not going to be broke anymore." That may have sounded foolish at the time, but I certainly have gotten to where I'm no longer broke! The change didn't come overnight, but making that decision in my head set the wheels in motion for the financial situation to change for me and my family.

Get in Your Zone

When you're focused on your own path, your mind is open to new ideas and revelations. Your limitless potential can be shaped by Destiny's unfettered hand. Those who avoid the lure of creativity are residents of the comfort zone. Those who like safety inhabit the comfort zone. The comfort zone is the land of the status quo, whose language is, "We've never done it that way before." Those words stop progress, stifle creativity, and halt innovation. Life in the comfort zone requires no challenge, no guts, and no determination. Everyone who lives in the comfort zone is expected to speak like others speak, do what others do, not do what others don't do. They choke creativity to what they can understand. The comfort zone looks easygoing, but it's tense and controlling. Residents of the comfort zone demand total allegiance. You can't live among them and dare to be different. You can't zip in the comfort zone, then out of it when you get a burst of creativity. You'll be punished for trying to live among them while they perceive you are simultaneously betraying them with your new ideas and originality.

Clusters of comfort zoners reside in every strata of life, from the deepest recesses of the inner city to the sprawling, manicured lawns of suburbia, at church and school, at your workplace and professional organizations. They're in your neighborhood, family, sorority, fraternity, and country club. They're among the "boyz in the hood" and the "billionaire boys club."

Young African Americans in urban areas across our country are often pressured to stay in the comfort zone of a limited existence of poverty and ignorance. They are susceptible to peer and even intrafamily pressure to not read books, speak Standard English, make good grades, or pursue a life that doesn't include prison or unwed early pregnancy. The comfort zone of their world says, "Historical racism and exclusion has shown us that you can't get ahead, so don't start acting like you have hope to make a better life for yourself." Beyond that comfort zone is a world of opportunity, Destiny for those willing to break out of their comfort zone.

Comfort zones don't have a favorite neighborhood. In the most prosperous neighborhoods, just as in ghettos, people are confined: marry only a certain type, enroll children only in certain schools, drive certain cars, shop in particular stores, maintain accepted political affiliations, and join specific types of organizations. Dare to think or behave differently and soon you must move on, an outcast from the comfort zone. The people who live there fear the noncompliant among them, fear creativity because out of its boundless abundance come visions and imaginings that cannot be contained or controlled.

Destiny seekers live in the creative zone without limits or boundaries. Their energies are stirred by the creative process. Creative zoners thrive on new ideas and designs. They await new expressions of imagination to energize and enliven them. Like comfort zone dwellers, creative zoners come from every walk of life, socioeconomic group, race, gender, and educational level. Arthur Fry, inventor of the Post-it note, had a successful career as an inventor and scientist, but he didn't dwell in the comfort zone of middle-aged, middle-class American males. His most popular invention spawned an entire industry that continues to evolve from its origins in 1975.

Daymond John, creator of the immensely successful FUBU line of urban apparel, rose from poverty to purpose by delving into his creative zone. He gives this advice to creative thinkers: "If nobody else likes it, it might be a hit." Since comfort zoners like sameness, if they find your ideas distasteful, that may be your green light to keep moving forward. Jump fully into the creative zone and you will find fulfillment and purpose that you cannot imagine as a comfort zone dweller. If you've been banned from the comfort zone of your friends, job, or neighborhood, say "Good-bye and good riddance!" Have the courage to walk away from them even if they scare you with warnings of dire consequences or potential pitfalls of taking risks and doing something differently. While Destiny calls you, friends, loved ones, and coworkers in the comfort zone will tell you to be afraid to go back to school, to fear quitting your job to start a business, or that you aren't creative enough to write music or plays or books.

Take on the challenge of seeing who you can become. Ignore the deceptive lure of the comfort zone. If Destiny is calling, you can never be satisfied with sameness and mediocrity. And if you're afraid to leave what you already know, think about this: If you have the courage to walk away from the familiar to pursue Destiny and it doesn't work out for you, you can always go back to that old place. Those same people you left will still be there when you get back.

You get to choose where you will dwell: comfort zone or creative zone. If you are brave enough to ignore the distractions, you will feel as if you have arrived home when you get to the creative zone that is your destiny. Your ideas will be embraced and celebrated.

An annual television concert called *Divas Live* featured some of the greatest vocalists of our day—Celine Dion, Gloria Estefan, Aretha Franklin, Shania Twain, Whitney Houston, Brandy, Cher, Tina Turner, and Mariah Carey. In session together, the divas were inspired by one another's vocal range and ability. That's how creative zones work. As you find your way out of the safety of sameness, you will link up with creative comrades who make you better as you make them better.

Finding your creative zone doesn't mean you sing or paint or sculpt or write or display any talents customarily defined as creative. The creative zone is simply the place where your uncharted journey to Destiny is free to explore all roads. Whatever your revealed purpose, you will be energized by opening your mind to ideas, and closing the narrow mental corridors of convention and sameness.

CHAPTER 15

Hear Destiny's Voice

Step Aside to Listen for Destiny's Authentic Call

I went to visit one of our church members who was incarcerated at a maximum-security facility for prisoners with emotional and mental dysfunction—schizophrenia, bipolar disorder, etc. As I passed through the corridors, one inmate introduced himself to me as God; others said they heard voices telling them to harm someone or to commit some terrible act. After the visit, I talked with my member's doctor and when she spoke about patients who hear voices, I told her, "Actually, there's really not much difference between what you do and what I do. We both deal with people who have problems and hear voices."

We all hear voices that can have an impact on our Destiny decisions. Voices that tell us, "You're not good enough," "You're wasting your time," "They'll never choose you," or "You're not going to get the job, so just skip the interview." Voices remind you of your past so that you continue to live in shame and fear of being exposed, a dangerous form of bondage that will cause you to let Destiny opportunities pass you by.

Sometimes the voices are old friends, alter egos—for example, the voice that tells you to give the boss a piece of your mind while you're standing in his face smiling. A voice tells you to quit when a situation gets too hard, to walk away from a spouse of thirty years, or to do something that goes against your values because "No one will ever find out." You meet a man or a woman for the first time and a voice says, "That's the one." We all hear voices. We have to decide which voices we will heed. Every day you choose which voices you will listen to. The voices that you pay attention to are the ones that will manifest in your life. If you've turned your heart and your head toward Destiny, train your mind to hear positive, affirming voices that offer wisdom.

Monitoring the voices you follow is critical. The internal voices you hear have to be brought under control because you carry those with you twenty-four hours a day. There is no escape from them. Those voices are with you while you're being interviewed for that dream job of a lifetime. Those voices speak while you're on a date with the person you hope may be the one you'll marry. You hear them when you look at yourself in the mirror, and again when you look at someone else and compare yourself to them. When you look at your bank balance you hear a voice. When you look at someone who seems to have it all you hear voices. Voices that say you're not enough can derail your destiny. But when you recognize that you have the power to change those voices, you can become unstoppable!

Internal streams of critical commentary can be empowering or damaging, but so can the voices of the people around you. External voices have the power to shape how you feel, what you do, everything about you—from your wardrobe to your career choice or the spouse you pick. Friends, loved ones, and even enemies influence us, but that doesn't mean their comments are relevant to your destiny.

When my oldest sons, twins Jamar and Jermaine, were younger, they told me how to put on a baseball cap: "No, Daddy! You can't wear the cap like that. That's not how they're wearing them anymore." So I curved the bill of the cap like they showed me and put it on my head, appropriately dressed to be seen in public. Years later, when my youngest son, Dexter, looked at my curved baseball cap, he said, "No, Daddy. You can't go out with me looking like that! The cap needs to be worn low and the brim needs to be straight." Twice I was influenced to change how I wear something as inconsequential as a hat by people who care about me.

We are swayed by other people's opinions about way more important life decisions. We've all made choices based on someone else's opinion whose voice mattered to us. It's good to seek the advice and wise counsel of the people you trust, but you can be so influenced by other voices that you might never reach your destiny.

If you're listening to those who say you should be a Harvard professor although you're a kindergarten teacher—and that is your destiny—you will not find satisfaction with your destiny until you close your ears to them.

You Can't Tell Everybody

One of the saddest realities we must face about life is that everybody is not going to be happy when we prosper. People haters can't stand your dreaming of a better life, despise your happiness, turn their nose up at you because you take extra care in your speech and appearance. They get angry when you find a better job or a new love. They stop speaking to you when you give up negative behaviors.

The more your dreams evolve into reality, the closer you get to Destiny, the greater target you become for the negative opinions of others. People who don't even know you may form impressions about who they think you are and what you do. They will critique whether you're qualified, intelligent, attractive, competent, sophisticated, or savvy enough for whatever you're doing. They'll always conclude that you're not enough and you have no business going after Destiny. You can't please a hater.

Haters are such an integral part of your journey forward that you can almost categorize them. Some say they can do whatever you've done better. Others minimize your accomplishments. There are critics of your desire to succeed who accuse you of being self-serving, dishonest, or immoral. And let's not forget those who throw up your past to discredit or disqualify you, reminding anyone who will listen what you did twenty years ago. But perhaps the most pain is inflicted by the haters who smile at you as they plot your demise. The vitriol of all these haters is nothing compared to the betrayal of one you loved and trusted and who claimed to care about you. Be strong enough to stand up again, even after haters make you drop to your knees.

All of that negative drama is enough to make you say to Destiny, "Never mind!" But don't you dare satisfy your haters by quitting. Make yourself happy by fulfilling your dream; there's no other path to success.

The road that gives you fulfillment, purpose, and joy as it takes you to Destiny is always peppered with jealous, envious, and angry people whose venomous darts are aimed squarely in your direction as you travel. The hurt may make you stumble, but don't stop and waste time on revenge or retaliation, or even reply, because the old saying is true: "Success is the best revenge."

A well-known comedian put it this way: "It's a hater's job to hate. It's what they do." That's true, but haters are also judgers and gossipers. Be sure to examine yourself so you don't begin doing what haters do. Avoid comparing yourself with others; saying you can better do what they do; putting down their accomplishments; criticizing their desire to succeed; calling out self-serving, dishonest, or immoral behavior; or bringing up their past. Gossip is hater activity. So is listening to gossip, which you can cut short by interrupting the gossiper with "I don't need to know" and steering the conversation to another subject. Seek your destiny, and do not worry about others. Only God knows the full story of everyone's destiny; you don't, so you're not equipped to judge. If you find yourself rooting against anyone's success, I encourage you to focus on yourself, what *you* do best, and march to your own destiny. Do not let yourself become a hater.

Before you get to the place that is calling you, recognize whom you can talk to about your destiny and whom you can't. Dream killers will question your ability, your preparation, and even your worthiness to live your dream. Their negative voices are always more than eager to offer an opinion. Often such disparaging commentary comes from those who have accomplished very little. They don't want you to, either.

Are you lagging behind in fulfilling your destiny because you're listening to negative voices? Learn to be selective about whom you share your dreams with. Some can't handle it. People with low aims can actually cause you to feel guilty or foolish for daring to have a dream. It's hard to dare for Destiny when everyone around you sees drug-dealing and prison as the predestined fate and a blue-collar union job is their dream ceiling. It's tough to be open about your destiny as a medical missionary when all your classmates are bragging about being recruited by top hospitals. It's scary to confess that your destiny is to marry the man you love and be a stay-at-home mother when your girlfriends talk about a woman's need to make her own money. Nothing is wrong with what they want. Nothing is wrong with what you want. That you dare to have different dreams can scare people, especially those in the comfort zone. When you encounter such reactions, make a mental note to protect your dream from such persons and understand the reason for their fright, anger, or intimidation has nothing to do with you or what you are destined to do.

Rather than sharing your dreams with people who can't understand or don't matter, spend time talking with yourself about what Destiny holds for your future. Hear your own voice affirm your vision. See yourself as prosperous before you get the money in the bank. No, don't buy things you can't afford. Relate to money as if you were rich. The wealthy, especially those who earned their money and were not born into it—tend to respect money and are good stewards of their resources. They are not often foolish with money. Affirm financial prosperity deep within you so you are already that rich person when you reach your financial destiny.

If you're not living your destiny as you journey, you won't be able to live it after you reach your destination. Destiny is not only a destination, a goal, a dream, a purpose; it is an inner process of becoming all you were meant to be. You are educated before you get the degree. Couples are married long before they reach the altar. You are the supervisor before you get the title. If you're not supervisor material, you still won't be one even after you get the job. If you're not good husband or wife material, you still won't be one even after you say "I do." Your mind is already where you were called to be while you await the actual fulfillment.

As you strive for Destiny, your vision may function at a higher level than your opportunity, which can create frustration. On the inside you can feel what is calling to you, yet nothing on the outside and no one validates your feeling. Hold your destiny close to your heart. Keep listening to your own voice. Hold on to your revelation. Avoid sharing your calling. Everyone is not worthy of knowing your inner voices; don't give the haters an opening to tear you down.

An Opinion Is Just That

People who knew me during my younger years would not have chosen me to do what God has positioned me to do. Back in West Virginia, when I was working in a chemical plant and preaching when opportunities arose, I would not have been the number one pick to have a thirty-thousand-member international ministry. Most would have expected me to take over my father's custodial services business. At every turn of my life people speculated how I would end up, what I would be or do. And most of the time they were wrong.

That's why opinions don't matter. Often God chooses the least likely to get the promotion, grant, spouse, or prize. Right now somebody doesn't think you're qualified to do what you're doing or have what you have. They don't think you're smart enough, wealthy enough, sexy enough, skinny enough, or friendly enough: a mother who doesn't think you're good enough to marry her son, a socialite who thinks you have no business coming to her gated community or doorman building, a business mogul who thinks your entrepreneurial ideas belong in the toilet. Their opinion is nothing more than their interpretation of you. They do not understand or know you, and they are not privy to your destiny. Allow yourself to listen to those voices and you'll spend a lifetime defending yourself and your actions. If they get wind of your Destiny vision, they are likely to say, "You, of all people, will never make it happen." That's their opinion. Ignore them. Your future depends solely on what God has created you to do.

I'm so glad I didn't pay attention to what other people might have said about my life and my chances for success!

Avoid the Deceptive Lure of Popularity

Opinions can be positive, too. It's wonderful to know that people are helped or pleased as you fulfill your destiny. Others can cheer you to great heights of adoration, but nobody can afford to get caught up in the high opinions of others. People will love you but can quickly turn against you. When you're positioned toward Destiny, don't get caught in the false lure of popularity. Develop a thick skin even when you're popular, and don't believe your own résumé. If you don't, it can later be painful to hear the voices of cruel, nonconstructive criticism. You cannot have it both ways: you can't choose to hear only the voices of those who adore you and shut down the voices of those who don't.

As you make your way to Destiny, you will learn much more from those who criticize you than those who adore you. I learned much about who I was from my haters when I came under a fire of criticism. The first time I had that experience, I couldn't even defend myself because I was shocked that people even cared enough about me to write about me, whether negative or not. I had no idea I was important enough to be hated on at that level. My haters taught me my own significance.

Your destiny doesn't depend on the opinions of haters—or applauders, either. They're all making judgments about your future based on your right now, and that's not a complete picture. Only God sees the big picture.

Don't Listen to People Who Have Nothing to Lose

James A. Baldwin said, "The most dangerous creation of any society is the man who has nothing to lose." Those who have nothing to lose don't care about their own success, so they certainly don't care about yours. It's disheartening to note the number of accomplished athletes, actors, and other famous people who have met with failure because they took the advice of someone who had nothing to lose.

Star college running back Maurice Clarett had great potential when a major NFL team drafted him. The young man had talent but was known for exhibiting bad behavior. Eventually, his poor choices led to an armed robbery conviction and a prison sentence. After he served his sentence, a sports reporter interviewed him about his experience and asked how many of the people he once associated with visited during his more than three years in prison. "None of them," he responded. "They took their behavior to the next person and wherever the next party was going on." But apparently, the young man engaged in some introspection during his incarceration. He began to understand why some professional athletes have a difficult time putting distance between themselves and those they knew—including family members—before landing six- or seven-figure rookie contracts. He observed, "You may feel guilty or feel they should enjoy this time with you because they've been around you. The truth is, they've been around, but they have not put in the same amount of work as you."

Survivor's guilt can affect those who successfully escape a life of poverty or dysfunction. Guilty for having worked their way out of those circumstances, they are tempted to bring along others they knew before who did none of the hard work, who are only interested in the perks of success, or who cannot leave inappropriate behavior behind. The successful are often accused of forgetting where they came from. They feel guilty and try to maintain friendships with people who are not going anywhere. Destiny does not require you to continue to surround yourself with people from a life you worked hard to escape.

A working but poor man grew tired of being trapped by the limited circumstances of his life. He took inventory of his friends and noted that one of them—who wasn't particularly smart or gifted—had amassed wealth. He asked this friend how he accrued his fortune. The wealthy friend's response was, "Keep the right company."

He observed that all his other friends hated hard work and had no desire to improve themselves. He decided to make new friends by attending conventions and seminars to connect with successful people. After he had completely replaced his network of friends, he made a list with two columns: those who would improve his life by association and those who could drag him down. Then he made two decisions: he would spend as much time as possible with the people who would improve his life; he would never spend more than five minutes around the people who could drag him down. After three years, the man was a millionaire!

Your associations don't have to be with the wealthy, powerful, or famous, but be intentional about associating with those determined to live a life of purpose. Of the persons you regularly spend time with, ask, "Does this person devote his/her time to helping humanity or tearing down humanity?" After giving yourself truthful answers, decide whether each relationship is beneficial to you in reaching your destiny.

Hear the Still, Small Voice of Destiny

A man who owned an icehouse lost a valuable watch amid all the sawdust inside. He made a thorough search of the building, carefully raking through the sawdust, but didn't find it. His workers looked also, but no one was able to find it. When the noon whistle blew, all the workers vacated the building to eat. While they were away, a boy who had heard about their unsuccessful search slipped inside the icehouse. He soon found the watch. Amazed, the owner asked him how he found it.

"It was simple," he explained. "I closed the door and lay down quietly in the sawdust. I just kept very still and soon I heard the watch ticking. I followed the sound until I found it."

Have you heard the sound of Destiny calling out to you? Or did you think you had been passed over? The beauty of Destiny is that there is a task for everyone. You are not forgotten or left out. Maybe you just have to get quiet and follow the sound of Destiny.

Life moves quickly, and most of the time noisily, too. The average person is processing a barrage of messages at any given moment during the day. You get up in the morning thinking about everything you have to do that day. Those thoughts race through your mind as you get dressed. You navigate daily rush-hour traffic while you listen to your favorite morning disc jockey or music CD. At the office, you hear voices throughout the workday, and as the day comes to a close you being thinking about your evening. And amid all of these messages, your mind is speaking to you about your kids, your 401(k), your mortgage, or your workout routine. How can you possibly hear the pull of your destiny?

Sometimes Destiny speaks quietly in subtle opportunities at the hands of those we least suspect. The ordinary-looking fellow you stand behind in the movie line may be the corporate executive who can hire or mentor you. Showing up at an event that is not a part of your usual social circle may introduce you to the people who will help usher you to another place along your Destiny journey.

Destiny is a powerful draw but will not overwhelm you with shouting. The quiet voice of your future tugs at you when you are in touch with the truth that you have a future and a purpose.

That voice can guide you. Connect with Destiny's unobtrusive voice and listen. Get quiet and still, like the boy who found the watch when no one else could. If you've never practiced getting still, discover the benefits of finding your quiet place. Develop a regular practice of stillness so that you can be attuned to Destiny speaking to you. Get to a quiet place through prayer or meditation or reflection. Use your quiet time to envision the life you desire. In that time of stillness, reflect on events and conversations that may be opportunities to move to another level. Think about how you are growing and emerging in preparation of what God has in store for you.

You hear sounds all day long each and every day, but Destiny's voice requires that you listen. You will find the message that Destiny has reserved just for you as you move beyond the physical act of taking in auditory stimuli to comprehending and responding to the message found within the sounds that you hear. Shhhh! Did you hear that? Destiny is speaking to you now.

CHAPTER 16

Exposed to Destiny

Step Boldly into Life's Adventures

The key to completing your journey to Destiny is to resist the urge to retreat into the familiar spaces of the past. In a new space, yesterday can look pretty good because it's familiar. But could you go back to yesterday, it would be not as warm, wonderful, and inviting as you think. You remember the comfort and security of the good old days, but if you went back to the home where you grew up, you'd probably find the rooms barely big enough to move around in, no kids playing kickball in the streets like you and your friends used to, and the nearest grocery store lacking your favorite brand of organic coffee. During an attack of loneliness, you want to go back to your old boyfriend, but remember: he's threatened by people who have more education than him, he brags about himself ad nauseam, and his mother controls every aspect of his life. Frustration with the feast-or-famine existence of starting a business makes you long for your old job's steady paycheck. But recall that the paycheck wasn't really that great, your boss criticized your reports, and the petty conversations in staff meetings made you want to scream.

Ignore the tendency to glamorize what you left behind. If the place you left had been all that great, you wouldn't have moved out of it to answer Destiny's call. Not yet arriving at your destination can cause you to glamorize even an unhappy past, and then to doubt where you are headed. You begin to wonder if you really have what it takes. Put that to rest right now. You have everything you need at the time you need it. Where you used to be does not indicate where you are going. You had what you needed for then and you have what you need now. You gained the lessons you needed from where you were then. Now it's time to move on.

Let go of what was in your past and let it stay there. Be thankful for the memories. Be grateful for the lessons learned, even the hard ones. Feel relief that the bad experiences are over and that you survived them. Keep moving, because you can't walk forward while looking back. There is so much more of life for Destiny to unfold to you. Give Destiny a chance. Make room for your present. You need all that energy you devote to glamorizing your past to learn the lessons you need to thrive in your present and excel in your future.

As uncomfortable as you may feel moving away from what's familiar, know that God is positioning you for a purpose, unfolding new places, people, and experiences. God's destiny for you is exciting and life-changing. Why try to go back?

Exposure Is Your Test-Drive for Destiny

Have you ever seen a car in a commercial or on a dealership lot and decided to take one for a drive to check it out? You look at the sticker price and then sit in the driver's seat. You drive it to see how it performs on the road. While you're test-driving, you think about how the seat feels and whether it has enough leg room. If the car meets all of your physical requirements, you inquire about financing and monthly payments. Then you make a decision whether or not to buy it. Maybe you can't afford the car, but just having the driving experience may be enough to motivate you to work harder to make the car yours someday. Or perhaps you decide that everything you've heard about the car is hype and you really don't like it.

Gaining exposure is like a test-drive on a car. You enter a new arena and you see if it fits. You see what it costs you to be in that environment and determine whether you want to pay the price. You make inquiries in your new environment, just like you would about the car, and find out all that you can. You have to work your way into the feel of what God is exposing you to, just like you work your way into the feel of a new car. You ask yourself, "Does this lifestyle fit me?" When it doesn't fit your needs or your self-image, you know to keep looking.

Destiny constantly gives us opportunities for exposure to the new, different, and greater. A powerful, pivotal catalyst for life change is exposure to new facts, ideas, cultures, languages, and information.

Exposure is empowering because it can mold, shape, and change you. You are the sum total of your exposure. You think the way you do based on what you've been exposed to. The foods you like are based on what you've been exposed to. The clothes you wear, even the way you wear your hair, is largely due to exposure.

Exposure broadens your thinking. You realize the world is much bigger than where you grew up, and that you can navigate that larger world. Exposure teaches you that there is more than one way of doing things and that there is not necessarily right or wrong, just different. For instance, after Americans visit other countries, they often remark, "Over there, they drive on the wrong side of the road." Actually, they drive on the opposite side of the road. The way traffic moves in England is not wrong; it is different from the United States. Exposure teaches you that many life decisions are about choosing differently rather than some universal imperative that requires people to live a certain way.

Those who have a great deal of exposure tend to be more open and less judgmental because they have chosen to challenge their thinking and make themselves vulnerable to new ideas and experiences.

But these are the very same reasons some people prefer not to be exposed to new thoughts or ideas. Exposure is a choice. You can choose to take the job offered to you in the international division of the company where you work or you can stay where you are—with the same people, living in the same house, eating the same foods, driving the same route to work every day.

But you don't have to travel halfway around the world to broaden your exposure. You can broaden yourself by taking a class in culinary arts or ballroom dancing or sculpting, learning a new language, or cultivating a new hobby. Exposing yourself to new knowledge and experiences is a choice that you make to not live in the confines that once nurtured you.

As already mentioned, once you are exposed to new ideas and experiences you're not going to be embraced by the camp that used to affirm you. Most won't have the capacity to cheer you on to learn more and do more. They'll say, "You're still going to school? You're going to be eighty years old before you get a degree!" Or "Why do you keep working like a slave for that job?" Or "You think you're too good for us now!" Use such disparaging commentary to motivate you out of the false comfort of mediocrity. Don't let their ignorance discourage you from pursuing Destiny. Make a conscious choice to surround yourself with people who make you want to step up your game, to learn more and to do better. Do try to bring along other willing minds when God blesses you with greater exposure. Share it with people who haven't had the benefit of your experience—for example, an up-and-coming young person. Just remember that is not the sole purpose of your exposure.

Exposure is all about conscious choices. It's easy to surround yourself with people who know less than you and who haven't had the benefit of your experiences. Those are not the relationships that pave your path to Destiny. The way to your future is revealed through your relationships with people who know more than you, those who've traveled to worlds you have never seen and whose lives have touched others in ways that you can only hope to.

When you choose to broaden your horizons, the price may be losing relationships, letting go of long-held family traditions, and feeling discomfort. You may feel like you don't fit anywhere: new situations are so unfamiliar and you've outgrown the old. You might worry about whether the new people you're meeting will accept you. Maybe you're not as good at this job or as talented as you think. Maybe they won't accept a woman in a supervisory position. Maybe your new in-laws will turn up their noses at you. Maybe your new neighbors will be stuck up or racist. You may have so many unfamiliar and unsettling feelings from this exposure that you will begin to think, "Maybe I made a mistake." You'll question yourself, "Maybe I don't belong in this world." And maybe you don't, but exposure is what teaches you whether you do or not. You may be experiencing anxiety from unfamiliar territory, or you may decide a thing is just not for you.

Part of the challenge to gaining more exposure is pushing past the feelings of discomfort as you acclimate to your new environment. Get comfortable with people addressing you as

Dr. __________. Become familiar with current events so you can join the dinner discussion at your future in-laws' house. Invest in an appropriate wardrobe for the kinds of events you will be required to attend so you won't be self-conscious. Relish the benefits of traveling on the company's private jet and the special privileges that come with your new dream job. It's all a part of your exposure.

When the discomfort of your new environment makes you fearful, ride the wave of feelings long enough to give it a good test-drive. Your initial fight-or-flight response may tell you to run for your life, but determine to engage your fight response and stay exposed to your new situation until your comfort level increases. Fight through feelings of inadequacy and own the new space.

Exposure also helps you know what you don't want. You may have dreamed of being famous, but when you're exposed to a brief look into the cost of fame, you may change your mind. You may decide you prefer the freedom to stroll in the mall uninterrupted and without an entourage and not mobbed by paparazzi or autograph seekers. You may have dreamed of being an investment portfolio manager, but once you are exposed to what really goes on in the industry, you may realize you have no patience for dealing with the whims and antics of trust-fund babies. You may have dreamed of getting a law degree and becoming a district attorney, but with a little exposure you discover you're better suited for corporate law. You may dream of owning your own business, but through exposure you discover the risks of self-employment do not, for you, match the rewards. Exposure can help you know where you fit or do not fit. That said, give the new arena time before you decide whether it's a fit. First impressions may be based on faulty or incomplete information.

It's wonderful that our postindustrial nation has grown to

allow us to gain exposure through more than one career. A couple of generations ago, a person who had several careers often was perceived as immature or unstable. Then, a person found a job or established a business and did only that for a lifetime. Now we think in terms of multiple streams of income, making money from various fields of endeavor. How do we decide to do this? Exposure. You may work as an accountant for a small corporation. Then, to express your creative side, you might have a small business as a wedding coordinator. You may also blog about dating and relationships. Exposure teaches you that you have multiple talents and can engage in many endeavors, even simultaneously.

Choosing exposure will require you to look at things differently and pay attention to life again. Engage. Read. Give. Pray. Act. Sacrifice. Think. Plan. Strategize. Assess. New experiences, new knowledge, and new environments can completely change your approach to life. Fear. Excitement. Anxiety. Nervousness. Restlessness. Insecurity. These feelings are the price of exposure. Whether you click with your new environment or not, your exposure to it is always a blessing. The fact that God has exposed you to something is always a sign that it can be yours. God is exposing you so you can absorb Destiny in the deepest part of your soul. Breathe in, breathe in and believe and let God open the doors to Destiny through exposure.

Destiny Comes in Pieces

Exposure to new thoughts and experiences is sometimes extremely uncomfortable for us because we fear the unknown new arena in which God places us. So God has to reveal our destiny to us in pieces. If God showed you what the Almighty really had in store for you right from the beginning, it might scare you into a corner from which you might never reappear. God created you and knows what you have the capacity to do—but you don't. You may see yourself as just a chemistry student or merely a mechanic. God sees the passion inside you that goes far beyond your present circumstances. God sees the great inventor, entrepreneur, physician, or teacher you can become in time. If God showed you what your Creator really sees in you, you probably couldn't handle it. So you get a little bit of it at a time. You have so much to learn along the journey that you receive it in stages.

When I was a boy, we played a game called "Mother, May I?" At some points, the child who was "Mother" would say, "Take three baby steps," or "Take a giant step." The child on the receiving end of the instruction had to first say, "Mother, may I?" before taking that step. In a similar way, it's important to gain direction from God to get to the next step. And as much as you would like to take a giant leap, sometimes God's instructions may be to take a couple of baby steps. You get a little bit at a time, like an infant who has just begun to tolerate solid food.

Sometimes you get exposed to the business as an intern before you ever begin the trek to become CEO. Perhaps your exposure to the life of a district attorney comes while you are working your way through law school. Your introduction to having your own landscaping business may begin with you cutting lawns in the neighborhood. Your career as a solo artist may launch with you singing in the church choir. Each opportunity then builds on the last until you become fully ready to stand in the position to which Destiny calls you. When Destiny unfolds rather than explodes in front of us, we can have a greater understanding of where we have been and where we are going. Having full knowledge of all the Almighty has in store for us would probably freak us out. The self we see now is not the person the Creator will shape to receive Destiny.

When I was a boy, I went to an event where my mother was speaking to a sorority group. They all knew me as Odith Jakes's son. Hearing my mother speak was exposure God gave me to a tiny glimpse of my future. After her speech, I told her, "Now they know me as your son, but one day they are going to know you as my mother." God showed me a piece of my destiny at that moment. I had no idea that the Potter's House was in my future, but I knew I would have an opportunity to speak to large groups of people.

Go with the Flow of Destiny

When Destiny is an adventure you can go along with that. But when Destiny threatens your job security or puts your financial resources at risk, it feels more like a nightmare. When Destiny looks damaging, be flexible enough to change so that at the right time, you will be positioned to get another step closer to where you need to be.

Going with the flow of Destiny doesn't mean you won't experience pain, hurt, anxiety, anger, and loss. It means you don't let it paralyze you and rob you of the opportunity for new life experiences and a new purpose.

When someone is dying, after all medical and all resuscitation efforts have failed, there is nothing you can do to stop it. Likewise when a baby is about to be born, when the water breaks and the mother goes into labor. The only action to take in those birth and death moments is to adapt and adjust to the situation.

Learn how to move on and find meaningful ways to fill the void the loss created in your life or stretch to accommodate the new member of the family. You don't do so in a day, or because you make a decision. It is a process. But when you keep moving with the flow you can craft a new way to find meaning in life.

The Mothers Against Drunk Driving (MADD) organization was founded by a mother whose daughter was killed by a drunk driver. This grieving mother found a way to keep moving in the flow of life, which no longer included her daughter, to find a new purpose for her own life.

If the company where you worked for twenty years shuts down, let it die and trust that Destiny is calling you into a new situation. When your marriage ends after all of your efforts to keep it alive, keep going with the flow of Destiny. When you realize a situation cannot be saved, let go and open yourself to the new opportunities.

Dr. Martin Luther King Jr. never intended or desired to be such a well-known or polarizing figure. In the mid-1950s, when black citizens in Montgomery, Alabama, formed the Montgomery Improvement Association, they needed a spokesman for their boycott of the city's bus transit system. The Montgomery pastors turned to the young, highly educated pastor who was fairly new to their community. Dr. King might have chosen a different life since he was educated at prestigious institutions, but leadership during the civil rights era was thrust upon him, a role that he reluctantly accepted but then fully embraced. Dr. King moved with the flow of Destiny and changed the course of a nation and the world.

When we choose to move with the flow of Destiny, we are trusting that God has purpose in the things that are born into and die from our lives. As we go with Destiny's flow, we will find a greater part of ourselves that has yet to be revealed.

When we are unable to move with the flow of our destiny, when the flow changes and we refuse to travel with it, we may find that we can no longer enjoy what used to bring us pleasure. We can't laugh at the things that we used to find funny.

We become dissatisfied with the things that used to bring contentment.

Life has many wonderful opportunities that do not come to us by foreknowledge or by any planning on our part. We must learn to go with the flow, even when it feels as if God has stirred up what once brought us assurance and peace. Destiny requires us to move on.

Look from Destiny's Perspective

Charles Swindoll has been attributed with this observation: "Life is ten percent what happens to me and ninety percent how I respond to it." The perspective you take on life's flow and transitions makes the critical difference.

Ronald Cotton spent thirty-five years in prison for a rape he did not commit. Exonerated by DNA evidence, Ronald and his accuser, Jennifer Thompson-Cannino, became close friends and even coauthored a book. But Joseph had made the decision to forgive Jennifer long before his release. "I couldn't carry on serving my time in the prison system holding grudges and thinking about retaliating against a person that made an honest mistake. I had to proceed on in life regardless." Perspective is why a man can spend decades in jail for a crime he did not commit and hold no ill will toward his accuser. The decision to proceed in life no matter what is why some thrive in transition, while others wither.

Perspective is how you view what happens to you. Perspective moves you to look at the rubble of devastation and see the phoenix rising up from it.

When people hear the word *grace*, they usually think of its meaning in religious terms, but grace also can be understood as a virtue or a disposition toward a thing. You can have a grace for doing something and then lose it, so your perspective changes. You can have the grace to work seventy-hour weeks and it doesn't bother you. You may even thrive on it. You may do this for a long time, then fall in love, marry, have children, and as you watch your children grow up far too quickly, you may lose your grace for working such long hours. Spending time with family becomes far more important.

Maybe you once had grace for putting out fires on the job but now have lost your grace for relentless pressure. As you are more exposed, your perspective changes. Through exposure you discover you don't have to live like you do now. Through exposure you discover you're worthy of a mate who respects you, and your perspective changes. Through exposure you realize that your talent can earn you a good living and great sense of fulfillment. Exposure changes your perspective.

If you are serious about Destiny, you will receive the gift of exposure and be willing to change your perspective. Through the ebbs and flows of life, through the challenges, the opportunities, the changed perspectives, welcome exposure to the new. You are meant to be there. Resist the urge to go back to what's familiar and remember that even if you do, what you left behind won't be the same now. Exposure has made you a different person who can't go back to the old situation. Focus on what lies ahead and then believe in God's power to take you there.

CHAPTER 17

Destiny Demands Courage

Your Steps Are Unstoppable!

It takes courage to produce what God is drawing out of you. It means you must rise to a higher level, an unknown place that offers no guarantees about what will happen when you get there. In a culture that worships success yet asks, "Who are *you* to think you can be successful?" it takes courage to believe you can contribute something. Who are you? You're not rich and neither is your daddy. You're not famous or powerful. Ads you see in the media say you are not good-looking. How dare you believe God has a fulfilling Destiny for you? Who are you to dream of success? Whatever success looks like for your life, my destiny is to confirm that the door to Destiny is open to anyone with the courage to knock.

Economic, commercial, and professional successes are ancillary to the journey to Destiny. Follow what you believe in and enjoy. Do not start on a quest to figure out the quickest way to fame and wealth. That's a critical point about Destiny. Yours may include fame, but fame is not the purpose of Destiny. Seek your destiny. Do not join the throng of thousands trying to be famous because they love fame—the adulation and attention that it brings. Those who enjoy enduring fame never sought fame for fame's sake. They were following a dream or a vision to accomplish something that drew them.

Take courage and figure out who you truly are—not what society, your parents, spouse, boss, or best friend want you to be. It takes courage to know thyself and say, "Who cares? I'm going for my destiny!"

Find the courage to walk through the rubble of broken relationships when you lose friends or suffer betrayal as you climb Destiny's ladder. It's painful. My own life experience is that while accolades come from newspapers and television, there's a private pain you must endure as people you loved, trusted, or admired turn against you in envy. It hurts to be criticized when you're trying your best. It stings deeply when you discover the insincerity of those you thought loved you; they only loved what you could do for them. It's a harsh reality to face that someone simply wants you to fail. You don't know why; they don't know why. They just can't stand the thought of you getting what you want out of life. But you cannot go through the Door of Destiny without passing through the Hall of Haters.

Be courageous enough to pursue Destiny. Stand up in this world occupied by more than seven billion people, and say, "I have a unique purpose and a destiny that is distinct from any other person who has ever lived." Know that you have a role, an idea, a plan, or a vision to make a contribution to humanity.

Have the courage to be uniquely you, to be different. It is easier and less stressful *not* to be successful, to be mediocre, *not* to make waves. No courage is required to be normal and fit in. If you are more concerned about people's opinion of you than God's vision for you, then neutralize what the Almighty created in you, give in to peer pressure, and fit in with everyone else: Dress like them. Act like them. Eat what they eat. Spend seventy hours a week watching television like they do. Live on credit, check to check, as they do, satisfied with barely getting by. Overspend like them. Go where they go. Think like they think. Talk like they talk.

Neutralize your divinely created uniqueness and you won't need courage. In this reality TV society we live in today, where the weak, watered-down, and mediocre is the standard, it takes courage to say, "I didn't come through all that I've been through to fit a definition of normalcy. I have the courage to go after my dream!" Be courageous enough to claim your right and affirm your ability to rise to greater heights. You're a rising star. You have inside you the courage and stamina to push away the negativity of conformity. Invite Destiny to come in.

It takes courage to be exceptional, wise, educated, beautiful, happy, spiritual, and knowledgeable because those are steps on the road to Destiny, a journey that starts *inside* you.

Being courageous doesn't mean you will never be afraid or doubt. Quite the contrary; the one who has courage gathers up the fear and keeps moving forward. Corral your fears and move ahead with courage, daring to be the human marvel God created you to be.

Don't Let Your Destiny Become a Horror Movie

Some people love horror movies. They tingle with fear or excitement as the protagonists struggle and strategize to survive. The modern horror flick can teach us a lot about Destiny.

Horror movie survivors are usually the most astute in the group. They are able to keep relatively calm during the crisis and stick with the strategy. If something goes wrong, they understand that the strategy has to change.

Those who survive to the closing credits understand that the only thing that matters is staying alive. If one in their core group of survivors gets bitten, they momentarily lament the loss and keep moving. There's no time to ask crazy questions: "God, why did they get bitten?" Neither do they feel guilty because somebody else got bitten and they didn't. They just keep it moving because they want to stay alive.

The path you travel to Destiny can create as much excitement and drama as a horror movie. You need courage to keep a level head and stick with your strategy, especially when you're under attack by some undead person who doesn't want you to succeed.

The protagonists in the horror movie have an advantage: whenever they are under attack ominous notes begin to play, signaling what's about to go down. Music comes to indicate trouble has arrived. You don't have the benefit of background music when drama unfolds in your life, but you can still keep your life from becoming a horror movie.

First, don't feed on drama. Stay calm. Horror movies are intended to be overly dramatic to entice your emotions. Notice, those who die in a horror flick are the ones who scream and freak out. They feed into the drama. When you are attacked on your Destiny journey, don't give in to that drama in your life.

Second, stay with the strategy. Be the protagonist in your own life script and calmly stick with your strategy. This book will equip you to craft a strategy for Destiny (but especially refer to Chapter Three) and God will let you know it's the right one for your life, if you seek your Creator. When you have a strategy to fulfill your life's purpose, you may have to make some adjustments as circumstances change, but stick with the plan.

Third, don't court the undead—even if the undead are those you love. The undead enjoy infecting other people and sucking life out of them. You don't have the luxury of hanging around people who have no purpose and have given up on bettering themselves.

Fourth, distinguish vampires from zombies. Understand what kind of undead is out to get you so you can devise a winning strategy. The classic vampire of the modern horror genre is smart, cunning, and physically attractive. When he comes after you, he'll usually be smooth, even charming. He studies his prey, chooses carefully, and lures you in before the strike. Vampires take longer to recognize because they are engaging and charismatic, and they may engross you in stimulating conversation. They are dangerous because, ultimately, they suck out your life force. They don't care about your hopes, dreams, or Destiny. They're predators who want to drain you dry.

Then there are zombies, the moronic undead. They don't think. They don't try to charm. They are simply flesh-eating predators. They operate in a perfunctory manner, simply seeking to devour living flesh. It doesn't matter if it's you or the person next to you. A zombie could be your best friend, mother, twin, or college roommate, but will still attack you.

Fifth, keep it moving. The journey to Destiny can operate like a horror movie script. You may have started out with a group of friends, fellow students, coworkers, or business partners who were determined to fulfill your purpose and live in Destiny. Along the way, some couldn't fend off attacks by the undead. But watch out, because that now-undead person you were once close to—dreamed dreams with, cast visions with, and planned Destiny with—could attack you!

Horror movie survivors keep moving in the midst of terror. They don't stop to ask why. Feelings of betrayal and hurt are natural responses when people or events wreak havoc on your Destiny journey, but bind your wounds and keep it moving. Glance back and cry for a bit, but you don't have a lot of time for whys. God owes you no explanation for allowing painful circumstances; God has only promised to be with us and provide comfort during those times. Rest in the assurance that God is with you. If you ask the person responsible for your trauma, he or she probably couldn't explain it. Just like the flesh-eating zombie or vampire pursues prey because that is its nature, the undead in your life derail your destiny because that's all they know to do.

A woman saw a dying baby rattlesnake, brought it home, and nursed it to health. When the snake returned to full force and vitality, he bit the woman. "Why?" the dying woman asked as the venom slowly infiltrated her bloodstream. "Why did you bite me when I took you in my home and cared for you until you got well? Is this how you repay me?" The rattlesnake replied calmly and dispassionately, "You knew I was a rattlesnake when you took me in." People do what they do. If you are courageous enough to keep moving toward Destiny, you will outgrow the need to ask why. Your why will be that you've become someone else. You've grown and expanded. Your thoughts, actions, needs, and desires now frighten stymied people, so they try to trip you up as you rise. Don't get distracted by them. Don't spend time wondering, "Why is she doing this to me?" Summon the courage within yourself to live the life you desire.

It takes courage to let go of limiting people, even when they hurt you and impede your destiny. You need courage to admit they're like vampires and zombies. Gather up your courage and let such relationships go, for Destiny's sake.

What Do You Do When the Theater Lights Go On?

You let out a sigh of relief when the drama is over. The last scene in the movie shows the lone survivor—worn, breathless, and perhaps a bit disoriented. When the horror movie has ended and the credits roll, we like to think that the protagonist has survived to live happily ever after. What really happens to the horror story's survivor when the movie is over? The vampires have been annihilated with a silver bullet. The zombies have all been obliterated. Along the way, friends who started in the fight have been lost. There is only one survivor who will go out into a different world without the people who shared in the struggle.

What do you do when you have survived all the challenges you faced to get ahead and there's no one left who understands the journey but you? All the buddies you started out with didn't survive. Most of the time people are so busy trying to make it that once they get there, the feelings of loneliness can become overwhelming. No one in your new world understands what it's like to survive on Ramen noodles just to get to your next financial aid check in college. No one in your new world grew up in the trailer park eating government cheese. None of your colleagues were taken to juvenile hall for engaging in gang warfare. When no one around you understands, with whom do you celebrate the victory against the overwhelming odds?

If you're lucky maybe you have a successful friend who made it through the horror movie–like drama of trying to get ahead. More than likely, there will be no one but you. The new life you have includes a spouse whose parents both have doctoral degrees. The college sweetheart with whom you vowed "It's you and me against the world" decided to opt out of the struggle long ago. She wasn't willing to wait it out for you to get ahead. Truthfully, she probably couldn't survive in your new world anyway.

The 1950s movie *When Worlds Collide* was a science-fiction drama about the catastrophic results of a new planet colliding with Earth. Your old world doesn't belong with your new world. As lonely as you may feel at times, remember that your new world is worthy of discovery. Meet the people in it. Savor the new experiences. Find fulfillment in the life Destiny has drawn you into. Your experiences have made you stronger, but they were not meant to define all of your life. Fill your loneliness with the spirit of an explorer. There's so much in your new world that you don't know. The people there may have a different history, but they have overcome their own challenges. You can learn from them, like them, and even find commonalities in your experiences.

There may always be a lonely spot in your heart from the drama you survived, but the totality of your life lived in Destiny will be more than enough to offer you the full life you desire. The decisions you made to help you become a survivor are the same skills that will help you find a comfortable place in your new world.

Make Destiny Decisions

Some decisions don't have an impact on your destiny. It won't matter whether you put on black socks or brown socks today. You can drive a red car or a silver one, a sedan or an SUV. Some decisions are inconsequential choices, so please don't place yourself under pressure by thinking every decision has to be carefully crafted lest your destiny be lost. Make the choices you want and enjoy your life.

But you *will* have to make some decisions that are pivotal to Destiny. These choices will make the critical difference between your ability to arrive at Destiny or not. These decisions will have an impact on the rest of your life.

Destiny decisions have a price. I'm not necessarily talking about a monetary cost, although financial choices often have an impact on Destiny. Most often the cost is courage in interpersonal relationships. It takes courage to make Destiny decisions. Courage to ignore what Grandma wants you to do with your life and choose Destiny. Your Destiny decision may cost you Uncle Willie's approval. Your Destiny choices may cause you to lose some people you regarded as friends.

What are you going to do with the life you have left? You may have fifty years or you may have two, but find the courage to make Destiny choices for the time you have.

Some are afraid to make decisions and they contemplate their options so long they miss their window of opportunity. They delay too long in making a decision. They could have purchased property at a great price after the housing bubble burst, but they missed their opportunity. They delayed investing in certain stocks and missed their opportunity before the market rebounded and prices got too high. They waited too late to launch a career or to bear children.

When you're so fearful that you're immobile, you can take too long to decide. If you make no decision, the door to Destiny may swing shut. You can take too long to ask the right woman to marry you. You can take too long to decide on a career change. You can take too long to decide to have children.

Fear can make you take too long to decide, but fear can also scare you into making decisions too fast. Figuratively, fear can make you grab the first train coming because you're afraid there won't be another, so you marry too soon, take the wrong job, or make a commitment before you're properly situated to honor it. When you make decisions too fast, you reflect back on your choices and say, "I wish I had known that before I decided to do what I did."

There is a critical correlation between Destiny and decisions. The decisions you make are the path to your destiny. Your decisions will lead you to your destiny. Putting great decisions in motion will change your life.

Sometimes it is not courage we lack to make a decision; it's information. Good information can bolster our courage to make Destiny decisions. It's terrifying to make a decision in the darkness of ignorance. You *should* be scared to make decisions with no information. Good information can unfreeze the paralysis of your mind to make a Destiny decision. Before you build a house, common sense says count the cost. You don't just start building a house without knowing how much time and money it will cost you. Whether you're quitting your job to return to school, changing careers, or changing your relationship status, get good information. Once solidly informed, make your Destiny decisions.

You can't make great decisions with erroneous information. I watched a television program one night about a judge who was about to rule on whether or not to extend a stay of execution for a man who was condemned to die by lethal injection. Everything was prepared for the execution. However, on the day before the scheduled execution, the condemned man's attorney presented new information to the judge. The information he provided changed the convicted man's life. With the new data the judge received, he spared the man's life. When you're about to make a Destiny decision, get all the accurate information you can. When you've got a good idea of what you're coming up against, you can muster the courage you need to keep going.

Stop using the excuse that you're waiting on God. Sometimes waiting is merely justification for inaction. You may be waiting on God while God is waiting on you! God has provided and prepared everything you need. He just needs you to take a step toward it. Get the best information you can and make a decision!

Sometimes we move timidly, as though there is only one precise step we can make, and if we don't make the right one, all of our hopes and dreams will collapse. That's simply not true.

Always strive to make your choices based on sound information, and then move forward. There will be times when you decide based on a hunch or a feeling. Pray about it and follow that choice. You will find that even when your decision was not the best, God can still use the situation to bless and propel you toward Destiny.

Elevate Your Mind to Destiny

Some are called to Destiny but never answer. They prefer to keep their heads down and live below Destiny level because Destiny requires showing courage in addition to changing, demonstrating vision, entering new arenas, stretching, growing, failing, and getting back up again.

You have to do some things to release what God has prepared for your life. It is not going to happen in spite of you; it will only happen because of you. Saying, "Whatever happens in my life is all right with me" is not choosing Destiny. Now is the time for you to make the decisions that will empower you to rise. God will give you glimpses of Destiny, but you may not know how to get there. When I was a boy, God began giving me peeks at my destiny, but I had no idea at the time how I would get there. I now can see how time and again I was elevated to a larger arena. Each time a place became confining, I was able to rise to another level. Each new level was bigger, so I could grow. As I arrived in those larger spaces, I had to learn new skills. In each new environment, I was able to order and steady my steps, gain new confidence, learn from new exposure, and absorb new knowledge.

At no stage of life should you be content to sit comfortably, thinking that you have arrived, that Destiny offers you no new vistas of opportunity, challenge, or growth. There is always another level to attain in some arena of life. God has created us humans as such fascinating creatures that we are able to grow on many different levels. You may have reached your highest economic Destiny but have not yet arrived at your highest level spiritually. You may still have room to grow to a level where you tune out the world's chatter to hear the voice of God speaking to you. You may have reached your professional Destiny but still have room to grow in your relationships. You can get to know your spouse, your children, your grandchildren, or even your parents in closer or more intimate ways.

Destiny is calling out to you. You are on the cusp of change. More is calling to you. You are not selfish. You are not ungrateful. You are not greedy. There really *is* more! You cannot stay where you are without feeling discontent. No matter where you are in pursuit of Destiny, get ready, get ready, get ready to elevate your mind to the high calling of Destiny.

Acknowledgments

The idea for *Destiny* crystallized as a continuation of *Instinct*, providing a thread through which to weave together two distinct but companion concepts.

In my previous book *Instinct* I shared how you are wired and provided strategies to unleash what God has already placed inside you. *Instinct* is the how, but *Destiny* reveals why you are wired. I felt particularly compelled to write this book because I believe the why is always more powerful than the how of life. I'm excited about this book as an opportunity to move beyond the how and explore the why. Both connect to direct you to Destiny.

The depth of my appreciation for the special people who invested in this project goes far beyond what the words written here could ever possibly express. From the moment this book was conceived, a multitude of people made sure that this work would come to life. Your timeless investment inspires me to continue to fulfill my purpose and destiny.

My ongoing gratitude to my publishing family at Hachette FaithWords, for their passionate efforts to make this book bigger and better than any of us dreamed. Thank you, Rolf Zettersten and the entire Hachette team, who embrace and support me and my work with the utmost respect. This book is better because of the editorial acumen and insight of Adrienne Ingrum.

Jan Miller and Shannon Marven at Dupree/Miller & Associates continue to amaze me with their tireless dedication and passionate partnership. I appreciate you and your team more than you know.

Special thanks to Olivia M. Cloud for your prolific literary experience. Your expert pushing and pulling helped me express my unique way with words—thank you, Olivia.

I want to thank all the faith leaders and pastors who have been so helpful to me down through the years in charting my course and fueling my vision with prayer and support. Thank you to my partners around the world, my Potter's House church family, and countless journalists, entertainers, actors, and business leaders who have found my literary work relevant to their lives!

I'm indebted to my team at TDJ Enterprises, especially Jamar Jakes and Zunoraine Holmes, who tirelessly labored to enhance this project with their insights and creativity. Thank you for helping me get my message out with excellence.

I have discovered what is most important: how to live intentionally and how to run with purpose. From my children I have learned to live and love much more deeply. I hope I have taught you that your greatest source of motivation is finding untapped the potential yet within you. Thank you, Jermaine, Jamar, Cora, Sarah, and Dexter for the privilege of watching you master your date with Destiny. I always say that Destiny leaves clues. My incredible wife, Serita, is who God gave me to reveal the beauty and lovingkindness of my life's journey. Honey, I can't write my Destiny story without you. You truly are the best! My love and thanks to you all!

Index

A
Ailes, Roger, 136–37
Alexander the Great, 23
Angelou, Maya, 8, 67, 189
Ashanti people, saying of, 79
"ask, seek, and knock" principle, 169
authenticity
  of life, 88
  of "more," 20–21
  of needs, 91
  of self, 7–9, 85–95
Azusa, 15

B
Baldwin, James A., 217
bootstrap people, 163–64
boxing, 82
Bridges, Ruby, 128
Brown, James, 8
Buscaglia, Leo, 9

C
Chadwick, Florence, 107–8
challenges and setbacks. *See also* failure
  as blessing in disguise, 150
  complexity of Destiny and, 143–45
  dealing with loss, 229–30
  example of Florence Chadwick, 107–8
  example of W. Mitchell, 180
  faith and, 67, 79, 111
  God and, 110–11, 150
  getting up and going forward, 180–84
  lessons of, 144–45
  making it through the storm, 108–12
  nearing Destiny and, 146–47
  relationships for affirmation during, 112
  secret storms, 109–10
  staying strong, 105–8
  story of the donkey in the well, 151
Chanel, Coco, 125
change, 66–69. *See also* decision-making
  comfort zone vs. creative zone, 204–7
  Destiny as provoking, 243–44
  feeling trapped, how to escape, 149–59
  flexibility and, 229–31
  letting go and, 68–69, 76, 145–47, 222, 225
  as test-drive for Destiny, 222–32
  when to fight or not, 75–77, 80, 81
Charles, Ray, 8, 97–98
Clarett, Maurice, 217
Columbus, Christopher, 21, 23
comrades, confidants, and constituents, 56–59
contentment
  life well-lived, 2, 3, 36, 53–54
  when to resist, 19, 188, 195, 243, 231
Cool Runnings (film), 6
Cotton, Ronald, 231

Index

courage, 3, 233–44
  to admit ignorance, 188, 191
  to follow God's destiny for you, 9, 17, 233–44
  horror movie survivors, lessons of, 235–38
  to leave your comfort zone, 206–7
  to seek knowledge, 194, 196
  to seek therapy, 104
  to survive broken relationships, 206, 234, 239
  to take the "chain off your brain," 101
creativity, 12, 27, 101
  comfort zone vs. creative zone, 204–7
  inspiration and, 27–29, 207
  taking the chain off your brain, 99–101
Crouch, Paul, 15–16

D
decision-making, 50
  about relationships, 55–56, 224–25
  Destiny decisions, 225, 240–43
  Destiny's perspective and, 231
  priorities and, 53
Destiny. *See also specific topics*
  "always pays its bills," 74–75
  approval by others and, 62
  being anointed and, 158
  challenges, setbacks, and, 24–27, 35, 81–83, 143–47, 183
  complexity of, 143–45
  courage for, 9, 17, 233–44
  crafting an environment for, 12
  curious mind and, 187–98
  as deliberate pursuit, 43–46
  distractions as holding you back from, 42–43, 44, 199–207
  as divinely orchestrated, 4, 13–17, 24, 27, 31, 44, 48, 57, 80, 90, 93, 99, 102, 111, 134–35, 153–57, 162, 183, 196, 197, 220, 227, 233, 234–35, 243
  drawing internally to find, 12–13
  endurance and, 77–78
  escaping life's traps and, 149–59
  exposure as test-drive for, 222–32
  failure and, 179–85
  faith and, 11, 103, 146
  focus on, 71–83
  following where God leads, 140–41
  as greatness, 63–65
  instinct, purpose, and, 9–12
  of Jakes, 16, 17, 100–101, 229
  the larger good and, 156, 200
  lifelong learning and, 168
  of Moses, 10
  motivation for seeking, 200–201
  moving from intention to inception, 11–12
  of Mrs. King, 2–3, 17
  ordering your steps toward, 33–52
  perspective of, 231–32
  preparation for, 157–59, 196
  prioritizing life for, 43–46, 47, 49, 52–69
  as a process, 121, 122, 153–54, 178, 183, 200, 201
  pull of, 14–17
  pursuing, 24–27, 36, 91
  revealed in pieces, 227–29
  risk-taking and, 192
  steering toward, 13–14, 87, 88, 105
  strategy for, 41, 151–58, 163, 182, 187, 199, 201–2, 235–38
  street cred for, 135–37
  synchronicity, serendipity, and, 14–16, 93, 146, 153, 157–58
  time and, 64–65, 119–21, 177–78
  as ultimate expression of authentic self, 85, 90
  as uniquely original, 28, 42, 132, 213, 233–34
  vision and, 38–43 (*see also* vision)
  voice of, listening to, 219–20
  what it is, 6–7, 10
  "whys" of life and, 6, 14
  as your *plus ultra*, 23
Deuteronomy 25:4, 56
distractions, 41–43, 199–207
Divas Live (TV show), 207
dreams, daydreams. *See* vision

E
eagle metaphors
forced to leave the nest, 51, 127
knowing how to soar, 30–31
Edison, Thomas, 181
Einstein, Albert, 25
emotions
of feeling trapped, 149
immobilizing fear, 241
overcoming fear, 184–85
resetting, 104
as saboteurs of Destiny, 202

F
failure, 179–85
fear of, 184
finding reward in, 182–85
getting up again, 180–82
faith, 11, 146
challenges, setbacks, and, 67–68, 79, 111
spiritual reset, 103
fame, 41–42, 226, 233, 234
Fenton, Peter, 165
finances
bankruptcy, 16, 25, 51–52, 109, 113, 116, 135, 161, 181
dealing with obstacle of, 149
getting in order, 30, 49
investing in yourself, 92–94
making decisions about, 56
mentor for, 176
prioritizing, 59–61, 62
flexibility, 66–69, 113, 141, 229
focus, 40–43, 49, 63, 71–83. *See also* priorities
choices and, 74–75
choosing your battles and, 75–77, 80, 81
on Destiny, 130–35
perseverance and, 79–81, 93–94, 98
self-care and, 81–83
stepping away from distractions, 199–207
to sustain passion, 77–78
time use and, 72–75
forgiveness, 190, 231
Fox News: Ailes Apprentice Program, 136–37
Frank, Anne, 128
Franklin, Aretha, 7–8
Franklin, Jentezen, 120
Freedom Riders, 144
Freeman, Morgan, 178
Frost, Robert, 8
Fry, Arthur, 206
fulfillment, 19–31
authentic more and, 20–21
challenges, setbacks, and, 24–27, 35
example of the eagle, 30–31
other people's dreams vs. your own, 90–91
other people's jealousies and, 212
other people's limitations and lack of, 22
plus ultra living and, 23
self-limitations and lack of, 21–23

G
gifts. *See* talent
God
answering prayers, 167
challenges, setbacks, and, 110–11, 150
as Creator, 9, 12, 17, 31, 37, 44, 85, 111, 126, 181, 200, 228, 236
Destiny and, 4, 13–17, 24, 27, 31, 40, 44, 48, 57, 80, 90, 93, 99, 102, 111, 134–35, 140–41, 153–57, 162, 183, 196, 197, 220, 227, 233, 234–35, 243
divine-human partnership, 11, 126, 153–57, 197, 238
empty vessels and, 68
expectations of, 9
faith in, maintaining, 67–68
fighting your battles, 77, 153–57
instinct and, 4, 5, 9
letting go and trusting, 68–69
omniscience of, 217
ordering life and, 34, 35, 37–40, 65–66

God (*Cont.*)
 purpose and, 19–20, 23, 85
 setbacks as divine setups, 68
 timing of, vs. your timing, 51–52, 126
 voice of, listening to, 203–4
Graham, Billy, 8, 180
gratitude, 19, 152, 158
greatness, 28, 63–65
 environment for, 99
Gutenberg, Johannes, 27

H
haters, 211–12, 213, 216, 234
Hell's Kitchen (TV show), 172
Henderson, Annie, 67
Hughes, Cathy, 25

I
I Had No Father but God (Crouch), 16
image, 60, 109–10, 179
inspiration, 31, 87, 132, 143, 157, 174, 207
 divinely inspired vision, 141
 Jakes and Crouch, 16
 jealousy transformed into, 42
 by people who help you spiral up, 27–29
instinct, 4–5
 authentic self and, 7–8
 Destiny and, 6–7, 9–11, 17
 God and, 4, 5, 9
 what it is, 4, 9
Instinct (Jakes), 5

J
Jackson, Michael, 8
Jakes, Odith, 36, 74, 118, 133, 175, 182–83, 229
Jakes, Thomas Dexter "T.D."
 addressing Ailes Apprentice Program students, 136
 assassination of Martin Luther King and, 94
 car repossessed and provision for his vision, 142
 childhood glimpses of his destiny, 243
 as choir director, lessons learned, 139
 church loan, challenge of getting, 79
 as counselor and pastor, 110
 cultural upbringing of, 133
 Destiny of, 16, 17, 100–101, 229
 dislike of heights, 185
 expectations of, by others, 215
 exposure to his destiny, 229
 father's lesson about finances, 133
 father's lesson about tenacity, 36
 in Ghana, 54
 God's order of life and, 37
 grandmother of, 67, 123
 hiring choices and staffing at Potter's House, 64–65, 166–67
 impatience of, 33, 37
 internal voice, changing of, 204
 meeting with Coretta Scott King, 1–3
 mother's death and, 118
 mother's driving instruction, 182–83
 poverty in childhood and, 132–33
 power of mind and childhood experience, 113–14
 prioritizing by, 40–41
 publication of first book, 92
 pull of Destiny and appearance on TBN, 15–16
 roles of, 40, 72
jealousy or envy, 42–43, 90, 110, 199, 200, 201, 212
John, Daymond, 206
Jordan, Michael, 4–5
joy, 4, 29, 46, 54, 144, 201, 212

K
Keane, Bil, 122
Keller, Helen, 98
Kennedy, John F., 169
King, Coretta Scott, 1–3, 15, 17, 144
King, Martin Luther, Jr., 2, 8, 94–95, 128, 230
Kluger, Jeffrey, 165

L
letting go
 of fight mode, 76

of the past, 222, 225
of some provisions for your vision, 145–47
what to let go of, 68–69
life. *See also* time
agendas of others, vs. yours, 61–62
authentic, 88
balance in, 29–30
challenges and setbacks, meeting, 66–69, 105–8, 146–47
comfort zone vs. creative zone of, 204–7
as complicated, 137–39
default settings, 102–3
Destiny's perspective and, 231–32
distractions in, 41–43, 44, 199–207
establishing personal rules for, 81–83, 104
existing vs. living, 45–46
expiration date, 127
exposure to Destiny, 222–32
feeling trapped, how to escape, 149–59
getting more from (fulfillment), 19–31
God's plan for you (life as divinely orchestrated), 48, 90, 153–57, 227–28, 233, 234
God's timing vs. your timing, 51–52
greatness vs. pettiness, focus and, 63–65
growth and learning, 168
hindsight and, 115–16
keeping your eyes on the road to Destiny and, 183
keeping your life from becoming a horror movie, 235–38
leaving situations and people behind, 50, 52, 54, 101, 147, 150, 199, 217–18, 225, 238, 239–40
living in the present, 117, 122
living your destiny, 214
minor issues, handling appropriately, 64
order in (steps), 33–52
prioritizing, 43–50, 52, 53–69
regrets in, 179–80
resetting, 97–114
reversion to past behaviors, 152, 221–22
risk-taking and, 192
role of past experiences, 132–35, 138–39, 194, 218
"shallow water blackout," 104
Socrates on, 86
when to fight or not, 75–77, 80, 81
"whys" of, 5–7, 13, 15
loss, dealing with, 67–68

M
Mandela, Nelson, 3, 143–45
Matthew 4:19, 165
McGraw, Phil "Dr. Phil," 164
mentors, 78, 136–37, 161–78, 201
age and, 177–78
benefits of, 174–75
biblical, 165
bootstrap people and, 163–64
discipleship and, 177
four-step approach to teacher-learner relationship, 164
how to acquire, 169–71
OJT (on-the-job training), 164, 171, 175
Oprah Winfrey as, 164
parenting as mentorship, 165–66
tour guide role of (as "mentour"), 172–76
types of specialized, 165, 166, 169
when you need a mentor, 167
who to choose, 162–63
widening your circle and, 168–69
in the workplace, 166–67, 171
Meyer, Joyce, 122–23
Milken, Michael, 103
mind (intellect), 13, 115
closed vs. open, 190
cravings for information, 194–96
depth of knowledge, 193–94
Destiny and the curious mind, 187–98
Destiny as starting in your head, 201–4
disciplining, 202

mind (*Cont.*)
elevating your mind to Destiny, 243–44
great mind vs. small thinking, 63–65
growth, and exposure to Destiny, 222–32
how to reset, 101–8
"I don't know" as powerful words, 190–91
knowledge and responsibility, 188–89
as personal war zone, 113
power of a changed mind, 114
protecting, 203
resetting your mindset, 97–114
stretching of, 190–93
taking the chain off your brain, 99–101
tunnel vision, 146
Mitchell, W., 180
money. *See* finances; wealth
Moses, 10
Moses, Grandma, 124
Mothers Against Drunk Driving (MADD), 230

N
Naomi (Biblical character), 123
ne plus ultra (no more beyond), 22–23

O
oak tree, 26
metaphor of acorn and, 39, 65–66
Obama, Barack, 121, 201
opportunity
missed, 115, 125, 241
recognizing, example of acorn vs. oak, 39, 65–66
synchronicity, serendipity, and, 14–16
using your gifts and, 130
order in life (steps), 33–52
challenges and setbacks, flexibility and, 66–69
creating readiness with, 33–35, 38, 39
establishing, 35–36
God's design for, 34, 35, 37–40, 65–66, 68
guiltless prioritization, 43–46
patience with the process, 37–40
personal strategy and, 41
prioritizing, focusing, ignoring, and, 40–43
resetting, 97–114
setbacks as divine setups, 68

P
Paige, Satchel, 125
passion (heart), 13, 199
patience, 27, 201, 226
Bible on, 136
with the process, 37–40, 162
Pearson, Carlton, 15
Perlman, Itzhak, 5
Perry, Tyler, 80–81, 171–72
perseverance, 79–81, 93–94, 98
Plato, 86
Potter's House, Dallas, Texas, 39–40, 64, 73, 139, 229
Prince (singer), 8
priorities, 40–50, 53–69
Destiny and, 43–46, 47, 49, 52–69
in finances, 59–61
great mind vs. small thinking, 63–65
guiltless prioritizing, 43–46, 47
in relationships, 54–59, 103
setting, 49, 52
what's important for you, 61–62
writing down, 44
Proverbs 18:16, 72
Psalm 37:23, 34
purpose, 4, 201
Destiny and, 6–7, 9–11
God's plan for you, 19–20, 23, 85, 230
patience and, 201
success as, 6

R
Radio One, 25
rattlesnake anecdote, 238
Ray (film), 8
relationships
adding new, 100, 103, 151, 168–71, 218, 240

agendas of others, vs. yours, 61–62, 100–101
anecdote of the rattlesnake, 238
avoidance of deceptive lure of popularity and, 216–17
comrades, 58–59
confidants, 56–57, 59
constituents, 57–59
courage to survive broken relationships, 234, 239
dysfunctional families, 88, 101–2, 189, 218
identifying type of, 58–59
mentors, 78, 136–37, 161–78, 201
negative associates, avoiding, 217–18
negative people, impact on vision, 22
negative voices and, 213–14
prioritizing, 54–59, 103
rethinking or leaving associations, 43, 47, 50, 52, 55, 56, 103, 140–41, 147, 150, 217–18, 225, 238
spiraling upward with, 27–29
supportive vs. non-supportive, 44–45, 56–58, 81, 112, 201, 224–25
"takers" and, 56, 74–75
time spent on, 54–55, 119
the "undead," avoiding, 236–37
widening your circle, 168–69
resetting your mind/life, 97–114
emotional reset, 104
how to reset, 101–8
new normal, 112–14
physical reset, 104
relax to reset, 104
social reset, 103
spiritual reset, 103
taking the chain off your brain, 99–101
Romans 8:28, 16
Roosevelt, Eleanor, 63
Rowling, J.K., 89

S
sacrifice, 36, 62, 78, 93, 144, 158, 227
Sanders, Harland, 178
Schieffer, Bob, 98
self (who you are)
alignment with your gift, 73
authentic, 7–9
distinguishing the past from, 88–89
distorted self-image, 99
"doing you," 85–95, 102–3
evolution of, in Destiny, 228
failure and, 182
"higher self," 87–88
investing in, 92–94
"know thyself," 86, 89, 90
metamorphosis of, 139–40
other people's dreams vs. your own, 90–91, 100–101
self-discovery, 86–89
as separate from your gift, 71–72
valuing yourself, 94
vision for, 99
self-esteem/self-worth, 72, 86, 94, 213, 232
Destiny and, 182
words "I don't know" and, 191
your gifts and, 75
Selma, Alabama, 144
Socrates, 86
steps. *See* order in life
strategy (for finding your destiny), 41, 151–52, 187, 199, 201–2
as divinely orchestrated, 153–57, 158
example, Jamaican bobsled team, 7
failure and, 182
keeping your life from becoming a horror movie, 235–38
mentors and, 163
Streisand, Barbra, 7–8
success, 14, 184
as authentic purpose, 6
as best revenge, 213
challenges, setbacks, and, 81
moving from survival to, 56
outward, 88
paying dues to achieve, 158–59
quick trip vs. slower journey, 119–21
"safe success," 179–80

Supremes (singing group), 180
Swindoll, Charles, 231

T
talent (gifts)
  anecdote of the "God-given gifts," 129–30
  authentic self and, 85
  God and, 4, 9
  instinct and, 4
  mentors for, 78
  obligation of, 200
  of others, response to, 199–200
  preparation for, 158–59
  self-worth and, 75
  separating your self from, 71–72
  sharing, 72–73
Thompson-Cannino, Jennifer, 231
time. *See also* focus
  aging, productivity, and Destiny, 122–25, 177–78
  bad investments with, 60
  choices about use of, 74–75, 77
  every day is a withdrawal approach, 116–17
  expending on Destiny vs. minor issues, 64–65
  fast pursuit of Destiny, dangers of, 119–21
  focus on Destiny, 119
  God's timing vs. your timing, 51–52, 126
  hindsight and, 115–16
  "leaving the nest," 127–28
  living in the present, 117, 122
  as priceless, 118
  protecting yours, 115–28
  relationships and, 54–55, 119
  savoring every moment, 121–22
  for self-care, 81–83, 104
  taking your eyes off the clock, 125–26
Trinity Broadcasting Network (TBN), 15, 16

V
vision, 31, 38–39, 50, 81, 129–47, 199
  affirming your own, 11–12, 214
  avoidance of sharing with the wrong people, 211–15
  belief in, 80–81
  choices and, 62
  as divinely planted, 31
  dream killers, 213
  dreams, daydreams, and, 31
  finances and, 60–61
  focusing on, 38–39
  following where God leads, 140–41
  frustration and, 215
  how to bring into reality, 40–43
  implementing, 35
  looking internally for, 12–13, 27
  mental blinkers and ability to focus, 130–35
  other people's dreams vs. your own, 90–91, 100–101
  others with, benefiting from, 29
  ownership of, 44
  prioritizing and, 44–45, 61–62
  provision for, 142–43, 145–47
  relationships and, 58–59, 81, 140–41
  staying the course, 107–8
voices
  of Destiny, 219–20
  haters, 211–12
  internal, 209–10, 214, 215
  opinions of others, 210–11, 215–18

W
wealth, 42, 89, 233
When Worlds Collide (film), 239–40
"whys" of life, 5–7, 13, 15
Wilder, Laura Ingalls, 125
Williams, Ted, 47–48
Winfrey, Oprah, 72, 89, 164, 189
Wittig, Joseph, 116
Woman Thou Art Loosed (Jakes), 92, 172

About the Author

T.D. Jakes is a #1 *New York Times* bestselling author of more than twenty-five books and is the CEO of TDJ Enterprises, LLP. He is the founder of the thirty-thousand-member Potter's House Church, and his television ministry program, *The Potter's Touch*, is watched by 3.3 million viewers every week. He has produced Grammy Award–winning music and such films as *Heaven Is For Real*, *Sparkle*, and *Jumping the Broom*. A master communicator, he hosts Megafest, Woman Thou Art Loosed, and other conferences attended by tens of thousands. T.D. Jakes lives in Dallas with his wife and five children. Visit www.tdjakes.com.